S0-AAD-115

Fishing the Connecticut and Rhode Island Coasts

BOB SAMPSON, JR.

BURFORD BOOKS

Copyright © 2003 by Bob Sampson
All Rights Reserved. No part of this book may be
reproduced in any manner without the express written
consent of the publisher, except in cases of brief excerpts
in critical reviews and articles. All inquiries should be
addressed to: Burford Books, Inc., P.O. Box 388,
Short Hills, NJ 07078

Printed in the United States of America

10   9   8   7   6   5   4   3

Library of Congress Cataloging-in-Publication Data
Sampson, Bob.
    Fishing the Connecticut and Rhode Island Coasts /
Bob Sampson.
            p.   cm.
    ISBN 1-58080-109-9 (pbk.)
    1. Saltwater fishing—Connecticut.   2. Saltwater fishing—
Rhode Island.   I. Title.

SH477.S26   2003
799.1'66146—dc21
2003001125

———————————

This book is dedicated to my wife Karen,
my kids Julie and Jared, fishing buddies Eric Covino,
and Bruce Guyot, who have always had a smile
(or were at least gritting their teeth)
whenever I cut into their fishing time to take a photograph.

———————————

CONTENTS

FOREWORD

I began fishing in the Thames River, and the waters from Groton Long Point to the Race, shortly after getting my driver's license at the age of 16. Since that time I've actively chased striped bass, fluke, and tuna from Cape Cod to western Long Island Sound, along with some exotics in South Carolina and Florida.

My freshwater angling adventures have ranged north and west to Lake of the Woods, Ontario and Gogama in Canada, east to the Maritimes, to some degree in all the New England states. Fishing many different techniques for a wide variety of species has become a lifelong adventure, one that has provided many valuable and unique angling lessons. I always try to take those lessons learned on one species or in one habitat and apply them to others, in order to put more bends in the old fishing rod. The result has been the evolution of a scientifically oriented, multi-species angler whose claim to angling fame is the fact that I've been skunked fishing for literally everything!

I graduated from college with a degree in fisheries management, which ultimately landed me a job with the state of Connecticut's DEP as their first marine recreational fisheries biologist. The years spent as professional fisheries biologist, working primarily on gathering information on the state's marine recreational fisheries, combined with my personal obsession with the sport of fishing, have provided me with some unique insights and experiences in the marine sportfishing scene throughout the region.

When I first began seriously chasing striped bass in the late 1960s and early 1970s, it was a time of plenty for most marine species in southern New England waters.

When I first started writing in 1972, reports of the jumbo cod and all the fish taken by local long-range headboats—which fished Coxes Ledge and the waters around Block Island—went from being a mainstay the first couple of years to almost nothing by the end of the decade.

Stripers were plentiful, with a higher percentage of huge fish in the annual catches than there are today. At the end of their decline, during this same time frame, when the last of the big bass were being taken from the population, many of the current IGFA line-class world records were set.

Bluefish were abundant and peaked in their regional abundance during the 1970s and early 1980s. During this same time, weakfish could be targeted with high expectation of success in places such as western Long Island Sound, Narragansett Bay, and Peconic Bay, Long Island. Schools of weakfish were cruising the Rhody coast and Long Island Sound often contributing to creels of anglers targeting blues and bass as incidental but welcome catches.

Fluke were abundant and a popular summertime species throughout the region. As with the bass, the fluke population contained many large old fish that were also setting records, some of which stand to this day.

Winter flounder could be caught by the bushel in those days, from all the coastal estuaries. Scup were everywhere and numerous enough that many anglers could catch all they wanted from the shore; they were so plentiful that they became a nuisance to fishermen seeking for fluke and other species. In those early days of my angling experiences, blackfish were plentiful and big, but only a handful of anglers targeted them, because there were so many easier-to-catch species available. During that same time period I speared a 15-pound behemoth tautog off Groton Long Point.

During the 1970s Long Island Sound filled with mackerel for a few weeks every spring, usually beginning around the third week or so in April. Pollack also entered Long Island Sound every spring, creating a fishery during May that was targeted by local party and charter boats.

Offshore fisheries were barely being exploited, except by commercial concerns. The population of giant bluefin tuna was large enough that the USATT (the now defunct United States Atlantic Tuna Tournament) was held at Point Judith, and the boats were restricted to fishing "inside" Block Island during the early 1970s.

Two somewhat recent additions to the region's angling menu—hickory shad and small "tunoids" (bonito and false albacore)—were around, but no one was talking about or fishing for either of them in those days. Schools of bonito and albies were generally around in late summer, but were not as well known or anticipated as they are today, so they were often mistaken for uncooperative bluefish. Only a handful of early saltwater fly rodders were intentionally looking for the bonito and albies beginning in the late 1970s.

Within two decades of graduating from college and the start of my fisheries biologist and writing careers, every species noted above (except the hickories and small tuna) had been either removed from the annual fishing menu or severely depleted from the population levels I experienced as a budding young marine angler. I had the displeasure of seeing all my favorite sportfish disappear due to overexploitation by both commercial and sportfishing.

Watching the demise of all these great fish while I was actively working on their management for the Connecticut DEP was especially disturbing. Fisheries managers at both the state and federal levels did not have the power and, hence, ability (and unfortunately in some cases the desire) to stand up to powerful commercial fishing lobbies. They lacked the support to pass the regulations and restrictions on commercial fishermen that were necessary to stop and reverse the downward spiral of all these species.

Commercial lobbies had—and to a large degree still do have—the ear of politicians (whom I believe should have nothing to do with the management of natural resources). In about two decades, their resistance to restrictions on the commercial fishermen drove every major fishery to rock bottom before the right things could be done.

Eventually, once the fisheries were collapsing and fishermen couldn't make ends meet, biologists and managers finally got their chance to impose the quotas, gear restrictions, fishing seasons, and closed areas on the commercial fishermen that were needed. At the same time, but with much less resistance, the necessary season closures, size limits, and creel restrictions were imposed on sportfishermen. The combined sacrifices of both groups have paid off in significant improvements of about half of the original fishing menu I began sampling back in the 1960s.

The future of marine sportfishing is bright, because these restrictions and quotas are working. As of this writing, striped bass, bluefish, scup, blackfish, and fluke have all recovered to some degree and are in pretty good shape. Maybe not back to historical levels, but the stocks have been improved, not only in number but in population structure as well. With each passing season more fish are being protected, which means they have the opportunity to mature and spawn a couple of times, with an increasingly larger portion growing old—which equates to *big*.

A healthy population of any species contains fish of all age and size classes, which greatly reduces the odds of overfishing and population crashes in the future. The ultimate result is better fishing for everyone who is out there on the water.

Cod, pollack, winter flounder, yellowtail flounder, weakfish, and tuna are still at low population levels. Weakfish, seabass, and blackfish are somewhere in between and showing signs of improvement. Some of these key species, such as cod, are at least stabilized and showing signs of recovery, while others, like winter flounder, remain in deplorable shape.

Whether you've fished during times of plenty, low numbers, or recovery, the fishing places remain the same. Every year the seasonal migrations through the region run like clockwork, with the fish traveling the same routes, feeding in the same areas, and holding on the same grounds to spawn, feed, and migrate as they have for eons. There are only slight variations in these patterns due to seasonal changes in water temperature and weather patterns.

Except for the fact that modern boats, electronics, and tackle have helped make anglers much more efficient and effective, the bass, blues, fluke, blackfish, and porgies are still in the same places they were when I caught my first ones more than three decades ago. Unless destroyed by man or nature, a productive fishing hole, drift, or reef is always going to be a great place to drop a line.

Over time, only some of the techniques and lures have changed (or rather evolved), because basic fishing methods are still the same; some are simply more complex or fancy in this day and age.

In this book I have tried to set the background by describing how the places and structures we all fish on came about in geological terms. Then, working from west to east, I have tried to identify, not all, but many of the more popular and productive fishing areas, not only from shore but also from those reefs and holes that are within normal cruising range of all the major ports and launch areas along the Connecticut and Rhode Island coasts. Included in this book are comments and sections on the offshore grounds of Block Island and Fishers Island, which eastern Connecticut and Rhode Island anglers consider to be part of their home states, despite the fact they were deeded to New York State in colonial times.

The primary focus here is from a light-tackle, multi-species-angler's point of view. The most important or useful fishing techniques, baits, and gear are used as examples of how best to approach each fishing scenario and area.

Modern lures, tackle, and fishing techniques are described where applicable, to help anglers who may wish to follow some of the advice in these pages become more successful in what may be new fishing areas. It is designed to be a tool for fishermen who wish to explore some new (to them) fishing grounds in these two states.

I have tried to point out the most important seasonal fisheries in chronological order, and describe how they relate to the natural fishing structure in a given area, for each of the major areas that are covered in these pages.

As long as commercial and recreational fisheries are sufficiently regulated—and the rules are not relaxed simply because a given species has recovered—the information in these pages should be as pertinent now—and far into the future—as it was before so many of the fish on the grand list of New England gamefish species were decimated by greed and overharvest.

To help in this effort, please practice catch-and-release fishing whenever possible, especially when it comes to releasing quality fish. It's better to kill and eat a few small keepers than a single big breeder. Remember to kill only what you need, not what you are allowed to catch, and our fisheries should be preserved permanently.

Tight lines.

—Bob Sampson
Salem, CT
March 2003

INTRODUCTION: A Geological Overview of the Region

The complex and varied structure of the entire New England coastline was molded by the meltback of the Wisconsin Glacier, which approximately 18,000 years ago covered most of North America with as much as half a mile of ice. When the Wisconsin Glacier was at its peak, so much of the earth's moisture was locked up in the continental ice caps that the water cycle was interrupted: The rain (or snow) evaporation cycle slowed down in the face of cold and a lack of available atmospheric moisture. So much moisture was held in the glaciers, and therefore not immediately recycled back into the world's oceans, that sea levels dropped to 300 yards lower than they are today. At that time surf fishermen would have been sledding for 15 to 20 miles south of what is today Long Island, on top of 1,000 feet of ice, before there would be any surf in which to cast! Odds are they would have been catching cod, pollack, and other cold-water species due to the general cooling of global climate regimes.

It was a completely different world than the one in which we live and fish today.

Due to melt-off and contact with the more moderate temperatures of the oceans, glaciers were thinner around their ends and were effectively stalled, bringing glacial till forward as if on

Jared Sampson and Jared Lamb teaming up to support a big blue one of them just landed in front of Race Rock Light. The current drift was so fast that by the time they landed the fish, the boat had drifted hundreds of yards from the lighthouse.

a conveyor belt along their undersides as they were pushed out to the sides from the incredible pressure of the thousands of feet of ice above. Glacial movement was much like a ball of clay being squashed down in the center, which spreads out at all sides.

As the Wisconsin Glacier spread out from its center point in the north, its edges reached the end of their movement, carrying tons of stone and silt along the surface of the earth. As the edges melted down and the pressure continued to push debris to those melting edges, this material was deposited along a defined ridge that ultimately became what is now Long Island, as well as high spots including Block Island, Martha's Vineyard, and possibly Nantucket Island—the end result of what geologists call the Ronkonkoma Moraine.

The glaciers melted back a few more miles and stalled again for hundreds of years, forming the Harbor Hill Moraine, which created the high grounds along the North Shore of Long Island—a string of islands leading from Orient Point to Watch

Hill that includes Plum Island, the Gull Islands, Fishers Island, and a portion of the southern Rhode Island coast leading southward from Narragansett Bay.

The meltback evidently took place quickly as the ice pulled across what is now Long Island Sound, probably being kept relatively open by stream flow and glacial outwash. Two more minor moraines were left behind off the Connecticut coast: The first, in Norwalk, created the Captain Islands and Norwalk Islands, then extended eastward far enough to create Falkner Island off Guilford; the second, called the Saybrook Moraine, includes much of the structure in the Madison/Saybrook area as well.

Many of the islands in eastern Connecticut (such as the Thimbles) are simply exposed bedrock that was swept clean and exposed by glacial action. They have been filled with silt between and around their edges, creating an area of excellent fishing structure in the process. Other reefs and ledges throughout the region were formed in the same manner.

While the Wisconsin Glacier was in full retreat, "Long Island Sound" was actually a freshwater lake roughly a third of its present size; it was maintained by fresh waters flowing in as the glaciers melted off to the north.

Ocean levels were still too low for salt water to have flooded the basin left between what is now Long Island and the Connecticut mainland. About 8,000 to 10,000 years ago, however, runoff from the then rapidly retreating continental glaciers raised ocean levels enough to mix with the fresh waters of "Long Island Sound Lake," ultimately filling the basin we now call Long Island Sound—including the terrific fishing structure that we all use and occasionally whack into with a propeller or skeg today.

Because of the constrictions created by those moraines that now bear names such as Plum Island, Fishers Island, the Sluiceway, Catumb Rock, and Watch Hill Reef—along with other major bits of angling structure that run diagonally across the mouth of Long Island Sound—some general tidal conditions are created that need to be kept in mind when fishing in the waters of Long Island Sound.

The average tidal range is much greater in western Long Island Sound than along the Rhode Island border in the east. For instance, Stamford has an average tidal fluctuation of roughly 7¼ feet, while at New London the average difference between high and low tide is only about 3 feet.

As you travel from west to east along the Connecticut coast, the shoreline becomes rockier, the bottom depths grow deeper, and the currents run stronger. In the Race, when the tides are at their peak, water flows at about 5 knots; it's 1 knot or so in the mid-Sound area, between New Haven and Bridgeport, and only half a knot mid-Sound off Stamford. Naturally, constrictions such as points, shoals, and narrows will accelerate the pace of water flowing through that area, creating a rip line—always a likely spot to catch fish.

In short, there are more places with fish-holding, lure-snagging structures and rip currents in eastern Connecticut than you'll find west of Middlesex County. This doesn't mean there aren't any productive fishing areas west of New Haven; they are simply fewer in number and more dispersed.

The number one problem in fishing the Connecticut and Rhode Island coasts is access. This book will look at the best public fishing spots, but anglers everywhere know that there are numerous local access points that are privately owned and cannot be advertised in any way. These are the fishing places people are allowed to fish discreetly—the ones that persistent and experienced anglers can sniff out by talking to local tackle shops or anglers, or simply by exploring the waterfront.

Major Features of Coastal Connecticut and Rhode Island

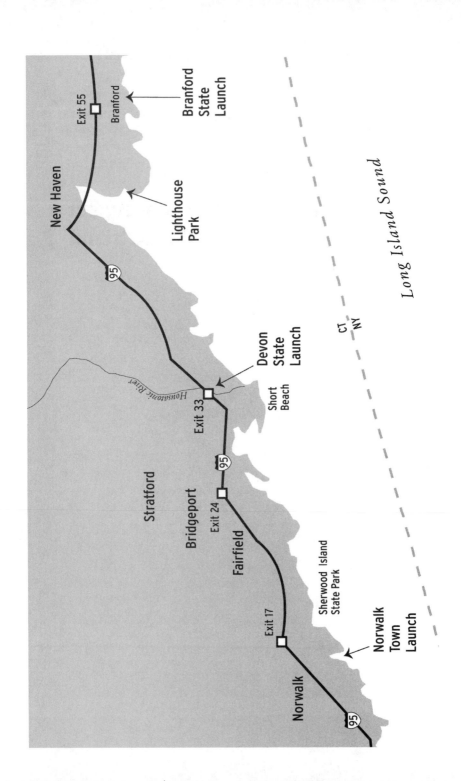

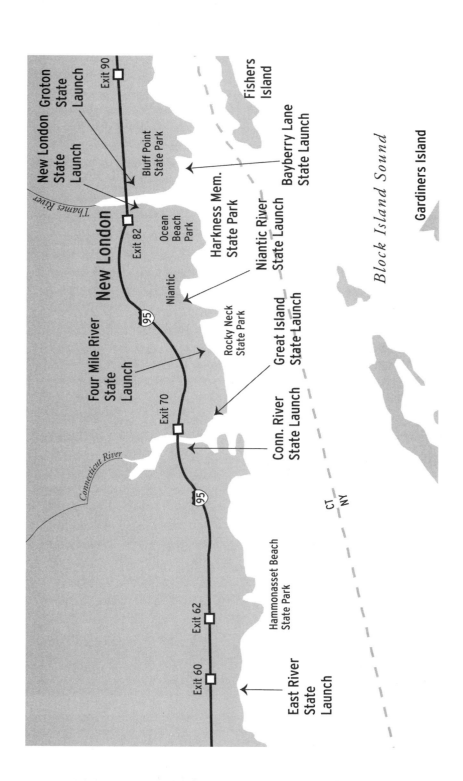

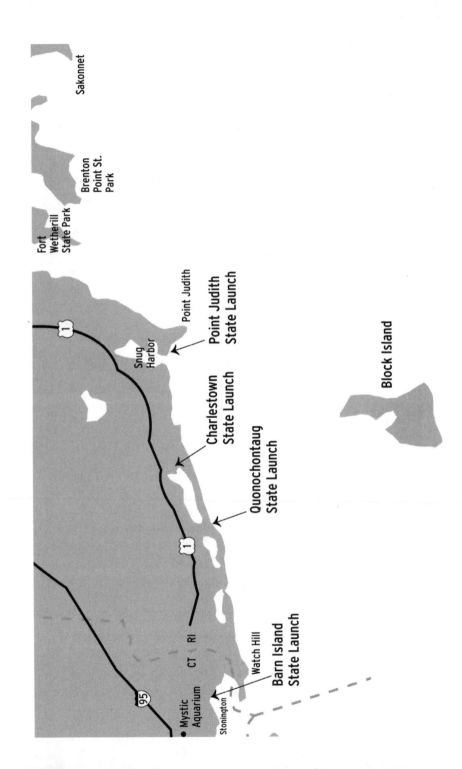

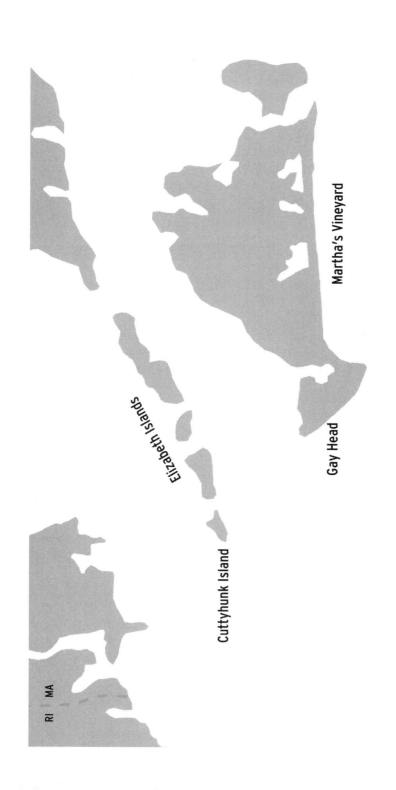

PART ONE
CONNECTICUT

1

Western Connecticut (Fairfield County)

THE NORWALK ISLANDS

Perhaps the greatest gift from the Wisconsin Glacier to anglers is the Norwalk Islands—a long cluster of islands, rocks, sandbars, and boulder piles ranging in size from prop-busting subsurface chunks of rock to 70-acre Chimon Island, the largest of the group.

Not only are the Norwalk Islands good-looking fishing grounds, but they also have the credentials to prove it in the form of numerous International Game Fish Association (IGFA) line-class world records. The 30-pound-test world record for striped bass, a monster 71½-pounder caught on a live bunker by John Baldino in 1980, is perhaps the most notable of these angling accomplishments. There are, however, also three world records in the 2-, 4-, and 8-pound-test categories for blackfish (tautog). These range from 9 pounds plus to 17 pounds, and all came from the Norwalk Islands—two from Sheffield Island alone.

The Norwalk River and Harbor lie inside the islands that are strung a mile or so outside this well-protected harbor. Striped bass, snapper blues, and adult bluefish chase bait—

often menhaden—well up inside the river, providing periods of pretty good fishing action that occurs primarily during the spring and late-summer/fall migratory periods.

In spring, when school bass are pouring out of the Hudson River and moving rapidly along the Connecticut coastline, they frequently run inside the Norwalk River to the first dam, giving anglers in the know an opportunity for some fast and furious plug casting or bait fishing on what can be easy-to-reach concentrations of fish.

Though there are some private, unmentionable spots along the river's course that locals utilize, there are two primary shore-based access points in Norwalk: Seaview Park in downtown Norwalk just south of the Route 136 bridge where it crosses the Norwalk River, and City Park at Calf Pasture Point, on the eastern edge of the river's mouth, at the end of Calf Pasture Point Road. Both places can be reached from exit 16 off I-95.

City Park, on the eastern side of the harbor's mouth, is located at Calf Pasture Point and has an excellent public fishing pier. People pay to park, but use of the pier is free. This is a fairly productive fishing spot throughout the season. Anglers pull some winter flounder over its rails in spring, though these have been rare since the late 1880s. Other catches include striped bass, fluke, porgies (scup), blackfish (tautog), sporadic weakfish, as well as snapper and adult bluefish later in summer and fall. It is one of western Long Island Sound's most productive public shore-based fishing hot spots.

Seaview Park, which is located conveniently across the road from a terrific bait-and-tackle shop, Fisherman's World, provides less consistent fishing—except during spring and fall, when school stripers and snapper blues abound.

Historically, anglers used to catch some winter flounder from the banks at the park itself in early spring. Nowadays winter flounder numbers are so low, particularly in western Long Island Sound, that few if any anglers target flatfish from this spot anymore. Still, when striped bass move into the river to feed during spring, you can take fish from the shore at Seaview Park as you move up and down the Norwalk River with the changing tides. Later in summer and fall snapper bluefish and occasional full-sized choppers, as well as striped bass on their return run to the Hudson River, are all taken from this public access area between late August and early December.

Both shore-based parks are best fished around the top of the tide and first of the ebb.

Seaview Park is also the location of the Norwalk Launch, an excellent and well-maintained multi-bay, town-owned launch site with ample parking. Parking fees are high—$20 per launch—for anyone living out of town. Still, this is a good investment for a day of potentially excellent angling. The Norwalk Town Launch opens up a water approach to the Norwalk Islands and points beyond.

Due to the fact the Norwalk Islands themselves provide the best fish-holding structure in the region, most anglers need not search beyond the channels and drop-offs they create. The extreme eastern and western ends of this island chain—Sheffield and Cockenoe Islands, respectively—are areas that produce consistently good catches of gamefish, including stripers, fluke, bluefish, porgies, and blackfish. In recent years weakfish have been moving back to more prominence on western Long Island Sound's fishing menu. The rocky habitat of this string of islands is great for weakfish. When they are in the area, they are often drawn to the islands, where anglers take them incidentally while fishing for striped bass and bluefish. Good fishing by trolling or with chunk baits for bluefish and striped bass can be found offshore from the islands around Buoy 26 and the Obstruction Buoy.

Anglers fishing the shallow, rocky Norwalk Islands have always trolled with sandworms for striped bass. Historically the lure was a classic Niantic Bay Spinner plus a single sandworm on a plain hook. Some simply set a whole live sandworm back on a hook and creep around the rocks with an electric motor. Both rigs are very effective when trolled around the Norwalk Islands and their channels. More recently tube and worm rigs have caught on and replaced the more traditional sandworm trolling. All work very well—not only in Norwalk but also anywhere that it's possible to run a boat near some rocks.

During cold-weather periods, anglers often start fishing inside the protection of the islands at the warm-water discharge flowing out of the Manresa Island Power Plant, located at the western end of the islands and inside the protection of the harbor.

When drifting in Connecticut waters is slow, fluke fishermen frequently make the short run across the Sound to the North Shore of Long Island, where they usually catch more and larger fluke along the golf course on Smithtown Bay and Mattatuck. The beaches and points on either side create some excellent sand-bottomed fluking grounds that many Connecticut anglers take advantage of. Before venturing into New York waters, be sure to know the various regulations for each species sought and for both states—and go with the lowest common denominator.

Within less than 10 miles west of Sheffield Island, you may want to explore prominent points such as Long Neck Point, Shippan Point (and Stamford Harbor), as well as Greenwich Point Park—all notorious for producing some jumbo striped bass every season. Shippan Point and Greenwich Point Park provide limited shore-based access at certain times of year, though Greenwich residents do as much as possible to keep nonresidents out of "their" beaches and parks. As this book was being written, Greenwich residents were trying to figure out how to keep the rest of the state out of Greenwich Point Park.

Shippan Point has some dead-end-road access points that you'll have to locate yourself. These provide great evening fishing destinations for surf fishermen tossing eels and chunk baits for big stripers. One friend, Fred Stunkel, a highly-skilled and successful angler, has caught fish pushing 50 pounds with chunk baits and live eels off Shippan Point.

The Norwalk Islands are one of western Long Island Sound's most productive—and popular—fishing areas. Anglers with time would be better served by locating other, less crowded fishing spots to the east. Boat anglers willing to pay the price will find crowded but excellent fishing in the waters of western Long Island Sound during much of the year. The western Sound's low point for striped bass production is reached during late summer every season, when water temperatures become uncomfortably high for the cool-loving stripers. At that time bluefish often take their place, with some huge ones coming in to feed on the ever-present bunker schools in this part of the Sound.

FAIRFIELD

Sherwood Island State Park

Sherwood Island State Park in Fairfield provides the westernmost coastal state access site in Connecticut. Take exit 18, the Sherwood Island exit, off I-95 and follow the signs.

Needless to say, with all the huge population centers nearby—including some migration from New York City—this is a very heavily used and crowded location. It's wisest to fish early or late in the day during the summer season, when interference and parking will be irritation factors.

Sherwood Point and the west jetty are open to fishing during the summer season; the entire beach is open during the off season. The jetty is the best area in the park to fish, with blackfish, striped bass, bluefish, porgies, fluke, and weakfish showing up throughout the season. Winter flounder are rare, though in the past flatfish were caught along the beach and from the jetty during early spring and again in fall.

The park charges reasonable parking fees, with variable rates for resident and nonresident parkgoers that differ between weekdays and weekends/holidays.

Penfield Reef

Perhaps the most productive (if hard-to-reach) public shore-fishing access point in the western third, or possibly western half, of Connecticut is Penfield Reef. It's located east and "around the corner" from Sherwood Island State Park in Fairfield, and accessed through a narrow, hard-to-find right-of-way between a couple of houses. Head south, toward the Sound, from exit 21 off I-95, then take a left onto Route 1 (the Boston Post Road) and, farther south, a right onto Reef Road. Penfield Reef is located where Reef Road makes a sharp right turn to the west. Look for the unmarked access. Parking is limited, but finding this place is a must for surf fishermen in western Long Island Sound. The easiest access—at the price of a longer walk—is through the Fairfield Pavilion, near Fairfield Beach off Fairfield Beach Road (a left turn off Reef Road). Simply park at the pavilion and walk over the dunes and west to the reef. On a good day the stripers and blues may greet you when you first reach the water.

The reef is a narrow spine of shallow water that extends about a mile out from Shoal Point, terminating in clusters of fish attracting and holding boulders with names such as the Cows, the Little Cows, and Black Rock.

Due to the large tidal fluctuation in this area, when the tide is out you can literally walk and fish the entire reef. Given the currents and rocky structure off its tip, Penfield Reef is a favorite among both surf fishermen and boat anglers, who cast in toward shore from the deep water.

In season this is a prime striped bass, bluefish, porgy, and blackfish spot that also gives up occasional weakfish. It yields some fluke and snapper blues in season, too. Most years, for a brief period in late summer and fall, anglers even hook into some false albacore, bonito, and occasionally Spanish mackerel. Unfortunately, like everywhere else, winter flounder have pretty much fallen off the fishing menu for this genuine fishing hot spot.

Penfield Reef is a popular fly-fishing destination, with anglers casting Clousers and herring fly patterns later in summer when peanut bunker are the dominant forage. Spin and bait casters will do well with chunk herring, chunk bunker, or live eels. Try using a live or fresh dead snapper blue during late summer. They make excellent bait, but don't overdo it—they are a bait to use when you're in a jam or looking for a deskunker. Some anglers fish the bottom with whole sandworms, while others troll with whole sandworms or tube and worm rigs along the rocks with great success. Poppers, shallow-running plugs, and swimming jigs such as Salt Shakers, Shad Bodies, and Fin-S fish all do well in this spot. Of course, the fact that the water here is shallow makes it a natural for Slug-Gos, Fin-S fish rigged without any weight or ahead of a light peg sinker to aid casting. Other soft plastics up to and including the 10-inch Fin-S fish are all excellent choices in this productive spot, where success is often a matter of "matching the hatch."

Ash Creek

Farther to the east, surf fishermen and fly rodders often concentrate their efforts in the estuary named Ash Creek, a series of channels and tide marshes that empties into the Sound between Penfield Reef and Black Rock Harbor, Bridgeport. Take exit 23 off I-95 and head east on Fairfield Avenue. Anglers fish the bridge on this road that crosses Ash Creek. Or you can head west on Fairfield Avenue, take a left (south) onto South Benson Road, and follow it to the end. By exploring the roads that encircle this creek complex, you can locate other smaller, out-of-the-way fishing spots.

Ash Creek is a popular fishing destination for many of the area's light-tackle and fly-rod fishermen, who catch school bass, snapper bluefish, and some larger blues when conditions are right. Like most other "dents" along the coast, it once produced some winter flounder, a fishery that is all but gone in small estuaries such as this. It is primarily used as a nighttime, dawn/dusk site by surf casters and fly fishermen during the spring schoolie run, late-summer months, and fall. There are times, when water temperatures are so high and bait is so minimal, that this area becomes nearly devoid of fish.

BRIDGEPORT

Though built up, heavily used, and polluted, Bridgeport Harbor provides a large percentage of the total miles of public shore-based angler access west of New Haven. Two town parks provide excellent angler access to the Sound: Seaside Park and Pleasure Beach, which stand on opposite sides of the harbor.

Pleasure Beach Park, located on the east side of Bridgeport Harbor, was an old amusement park that has been proposed as a site for yet another casino, though for the time being it's just a run-down fishing pier and classic beachfront. Large angler-accessible jetties protect the main channel leading into Bridgeport Harbor. On a map they look like the valves of a heart, bending open to the Sound.

Seaside Park, on the western side of the harbor, provides a long coastline from which to fish. You can get to the park by following signs to the University of Bridgeport from exit 27. The main thoroughfare into the campus is Park Avenue. At the end of Park Avenue, take a right at the T and pick up any of the roads that head toward the water. Waldmere Avenue heads west and blends into Barnum Boulevard, which runs around the perimeter of the park to all the potential fishing places. At the western end of the park is Fayerweather Island, a rocky spit that runs along the edge of Black Rock Harbor (one of the most highly polluted areas along the Connecticut coast).

Fayerweather Island is a good fishing place that produces blackfish, striped bass, bluefish, porgies, snapper blues, and weakfish when they are in the harbor chasing bunker. The rocks can be slippery, and the narrow spit that connects it to

Bridgeport Harbor as seen heading east. Fayerweather Island is at bottom, the mouth of the Housatonic River at top. Despite all the pollution and human interference, the beaches and harbors in this area all produce some great striper and bluefish action.

the shore can flood on high tides, but the long walk is often worth it when fish are in the area.

At the eastern end of Seaside Park you can walk out along treacherous rocks to reach the long jetty during low tide and fish your way out to the end. Bear in mind that the rocks are flooded at high tide, occasionally trapping anglers on the jetty for a tidal cycle, unless they wish to get wet and swim back to shore. Many a fisherman has miscalculated the tide or lost track of time due to a hot bite from bluefish, stripers, blackfish, or porgies at the far end from shore and become stuck or forced to get wet in order to get back to land.

On the eastern side of Bridgeport Harbor is spacious Pleasure Beach Park, easily reached from exit 30 off I-95. Head west into Bridgeport, take a left (south) turn onto Central Avenue, and follow it straight down to the water and over the wooden bridge across Lewis Gut to the park, which is isolated at the western end of a long, sandy barrier beach.

Rick Rinaldi with a 7-pound blackfish, caught in November off a large pier in New London Harbor, proof that more restrictive regulations can help. These fish can be caught around any pier, jetty, rock pile, or deep-water rock structure in the region from October through late November.

At Pleasure Beach you'll find a fairly productive fishing pier with easy access that may even be accessible to handicapped fishermen. More adventurous anglers will park on the beach and walk the half mile of rocks to fish at the end of this productive jetty. This one does not trap anglers because it has a dry connection to the shore.

When tides are moving, both jetties are very productive fishing destinations, particularly when stripers and bluefish are pushing bait along the shoreline. Bridgeport Harbor often attracts large schools of menhaden in summer. Anglers fishing the jetties when the bunker are swimming through are usually prepared to snag one or two for fresh-cut bait, or to send a live one back out with a hook for the big stripers and bluefish that are usually pushing this important bait source. The jetties are also a primary fishing destination for local anglers, who target porgies, tautog, fluke, and snapper blues for the table when these species are in season.

To the east, along the outer side of the beach, look for a series of fish-holding jetties that stick out into the essentially barren sandy shoreline from Long Beach to Lordship Beach and the mouth of the Housatonic River. This series of rock structures in a sandy world are the spots to target when casting with plugs from shore or boat, particularly when the tide is high and dropping.

2

The Housatonic River and Stratford Point

Wherever a coastal river merges with the ocean it creates an environment with an abundance and variety of food sources, which in turn makes for a great fishing spot. The Housatonic River is the westernmost of Connecticut's three largest rivers.

The Housey cuts its course along the western third of the state, finally emptying into Long Island Sound between Crimbo Point, Stratford, and Milford Point, Milford, creating an extensive series of tide marshes along its eastern side. Here the dry land of Milford Point shelters these delicate wonders of nature from the open Sound, creating the Nells Island Marsh.

The foods available in this complex natural system include herring, shad, and menhaden—adults and juveniles. Hickory shad adults, adult menhaden, and the normal tide-marsh species such as silversides, mummichogs, anchovies, eels, shrimp, crabs, and a variety of sandworms are all found in tidal marshes and estuaries sometime during the year. It is a veritable smorgasbord for the various predatory fish that move into and out of the area with tides, prevailing river flows, and temperature regimes.

In addition to the natural fish attractants in this river is the Devon Power Plant, which lies in the lower stretch of the Housey just above the Nells Island Marsh. Its warm-water outflow creates some excellent fishing, particularly during cool- and cold-water periods of fall, winter, and early spring. Devon is a place that normally produces striper catches throughout winter, with prime fishing taking place during April/May, then again from October through December.

Anglers cast swimming plugs, jigs, soft plastics, chunk baits, and sandworms either from shore or from small boats anchored in the river in front of the discharge canal.

During spring, usually beginning in April and running through May, there is a herring run into the Housatonic River that attracts some pretty large stripers up as far inland as the Derby Dam, where the carnage takes place.

Hickory shad have come on very strong throughout the region over the past 10 years. Once somewhat rare, now they are found in most marine estuaries beginning sometime in spring and lasting until fall.

As of spring 2002 a statewide ban on the taking of herring was in place. For this reason the live herring fishery that would normally be going on at the major dams throughout the state during late April and early May has been put on hold. In the absence of live baits, frozen cut baits or large herringlike lures such as Mambo Minnows, 10-inch-long Fin-S fish, or 9-inch Slug-Gos will do the trick when herring are being chased by jumbo bass and alewives are illegal to use. (This regulation is likely to change with time, so check the current *Connecticut Anglers Guide* or local shops to be sure of its current status.)

By mid- to late April the migration of striped bass out of the Hudson River usually hits full speed ahead, which means fishing activity for small schoolie bass in the 20-inch range peaks in the lower Housatonic River and adjacent shorelines. Exactly when this happens is dependent on when that magical 50-degree surface water temperature is achieved. Anglers do well on schoolies by casting small narrow-profile lures in the 5-inch size range such as shallow and suspending Rapalas, Husky Jerks, Redfins, Bomber Shallow Runners, Slug-Gos, Fin-S fish cast weightless on a 2/0 or 3/0 Texposer hook, and swimming jigs such as Salt Shakers and Shad Bodies on triangular jigheads.

The rocks off the old Remington Gun Club at Stratford Point have long produced some of the largest stripers caught in this area every season. This is a great starting point at any time or tide, but high water with a dropping tide is usually the best time to fish this and adjacent areas for bass. You can fish up inside the Housatonic River mouth at Short Beach and follow the fish as they drop downriver past Stratford Point.

On the Sound side of the point lie Long Beach, Point No Point, and Lordship Beach, all located east of the Pleasure Beach access area. A series of short jetties along the shore make great striper-holding structures in a generally barren shoreline. When fish are in the area and pushing bait, you can "hopscotch" from spot to spot, by car or on foot, chasing the fish in whichever direction the tide is dragging them.

Upriver, other angler access points include the Stratford Town Launch Area off Ferry Road, which runs along the west side of the Housey before linking up with Stratford Avenue. Boaters will pay a fee to launch here. A mile upriver are the Washington Street bridge and I-95 Devon bridge overpasses, both of which create fish-holding structure around their abutments for fishing from shore or boat. You can feel your way along the river from the launch all the way around Stratford Point to Long Beach. Be aware that much of the area is private and access points are not well marked.

Boat anglers can pay to launch at the Stratford Town Launch Area or launch for free at the often crowded Devon State Launch Area. Take exit 34 off I-95 and head west on Route 1, turning north onto Naugatuck Avenue; the launch is on the left under the highway bridge. It is possible to find your way to this launch by keeping in mind where the I-95 bridge is over the Housatonic River—the launch is literally under the bridge. (As a general rule, look for state access areas or launch sites under nearly all the places where I-95 crosses a river.) There is free access for up to 80 cars. Get there early on weekends; this popular site fills up quickly.

In spring the river itself is loaded with bass, and blues with snappers joining them in late summer and fall. Summertime anglers drift for fluke in the lower river, around the mouth of the Housatonic or off the beaches on either side leading toward Bridgeport to the west or Milford to the east.

Off the mouth of the Housey, the bottom is sculpted into a series of deep ripples, angling to the west from the river mouth. Gamefish often collect in the troughs created between the high spots. Over the years my friends and I have caught weakfish, fluke, stripers, and bluefish in this area. When weakfish (which have been making a minor comeback in Connecticut waters since the mid-1990s) are in the area, these ripples in the sand bottom, in 15 to 25 feet of water, are a concentration point that anglers in the know focus on when hunting for fish.

Same with fluke. These aggressive gamefish are attracted to the abundance of food constantly flowing out of the river and set up to ambush their meals in the troughs off its mouth. A popular and productive method of catching both weaks and fluke is to drift small bucktails or soft plastic jigs tipped with strips of squid and a live mummichog. Both species will whack this rig, which for years has jokingly been called a fluke sandwich. Fly rodders use a short section of lead-core line between their leader and their sinking fly line as a superfast-sinking tippet, then drift Deceivers, squid flies, or other small offerings to catch fluke, weakfish, and striped bass.

3

Middle Connecticut (New Haven and Middlesex Counties)

CHARLES ISLAND AND MILFORD HARBOR

Another bit of classic structure caused by tidal movements—it's very similar in nature to Penfield Reef—is Charles Island, located on Silver Sands State Park, Milford. From exit 35 off I-95, take Seaside Avenue to Broadway Street; bingo, it's there. Parking is free, and the fishing is excellent—some of the best in this part of the state.

This rivals Penfield Reef as the best shore-fishing destination west of the Connecticut River. Jutting out from the sandy shoreline like a lollipop, Charles Island itself is connected to the mainland at low tide by a narrow ribbon, or tombolo, which extends roughly a mile off the shore.

At low tide you can walk to the island and fish the 7- to 20-foot drop-offs that are within casting distance of its perimeter. When the tides are moving in either direction and "the Bar" is awash with fast-running water, however, it becomes a treacherous spot, so you must be aware of the tides and time required to make it back to the mainland (unless you plan to spend an extra six or eight hours fishing from the high ground of the island). Wear an inflatable life jacket when fishing the end of the island, especially after dark.

This is such a fishy spot because of its location between Milford Pointon the mouth of the Housatonic River, Milford Harbor, and the Milford Gulf, which is essentially a large pocket along the shoreline bounded by dry land on three sides at dead low tide. It is a natural fish-gathering area that attracts all varieties of gamefish, including striped bass, bluefish, weakfish, fluke, and winter flounder during the cold-water season; hickory shad from spring through early fall; and small tuna, usually false albacore, when they are around the area late in the summer and fall.

The gulf is a place that naturally collects schools of bait, including both adult and peanut bunker when they are in the area. The narrow and slightly deeper Milford Harbor itself draws bass, bluefish, and snapper blues up through its narrow opening to the Sound. Anglers line up on the jetty and access areas near the harbor mouth to catch snapper bluefish in late summer. Early and late in the day from early spring to late fall, these same spots become prime striper and bluefish spots for surf casters who toss chunk baits, live menhaden, and hickory shad. Multihook snapper rigs or snapper poppers—those float rigs with a single small tube 2 feet below—are killer snapper baits ready-made to be fished in this spot. All the classic lures, including soft plastics, shallow swimmers, poppers, and flies, can be put to use. An energetic angler can follow the movement of fish out of Milford Harbor and along Gulf Beach on the ebb tide or up and across the bar at Charles Island on the flood, with only a short car ride in between. This is not just a "schoolie bass spot"; 50-pounders have been caught up inside the harbor and gulf.

Boat fishermen departing from the Devon State Launch on the Housey often make the short run to fish the deeper waters along the drop-off on the seaward side of the Milford Gulf, from Charles Island to Welches Point. The primary destination is the water off the tip of Charles Island, especially on the high tide, when many surf casters vacate the island. The rocks that drop-off into 30 feet of water here are among the few bits of solid fish-holding structure in this very sandy stretch of Connecticut coastline.

NEW HAVEN HARBOR

Created by the confluence of the Quinnipiac River with Long Island Sound, New Haven Harbor is a very shallow, sand-flat-lined, filthy, industrialized port with a small, but very active contingent of lobster boats and trawlers. Though a good fishing area at times, it certainly does not draw anglers from around the region: Most are local who drive from their homes and fish for the freezer. Still, the locals who know the places to fish and what tides to fish them do quite well.

Shore fishing is hampered by the extensive, shallow flats that dominate the structure throughout most of the lower harbor—though anglers fishing from boats do very well on bass, bluefish, blackfish, and fluke around the three large offshore breakwalls that guard the harbor entrance a mile or so out into the Sound. Shore-based anglers need to wait for high water, or wade as far out onto the flats as they can and cast into the deeper waters where cuts are created by moving water.

Perhaps the most notable of the catches made in this area is the current Connecticut-record striped bass, a monster 75-pound, 6-ounce brute that was caught by Steven Franco on a live menhaden during the spring/early-summer period in 1992. The fish was probably of Hudson River origin, based on the timing and location of this catch, though no method is available (other than expensive DNA testing) to positively separate Hudson River from the southern stocks of fish.

On the western side of the harbor mouth lies Savin Rock, with a string of shallow-water public fishing piers that occasionally produce fish on the flood tide. Angling into the harbor lies a long, shallow sand spit known as Sandy Point. Anglers will occasionally wade out to its tip and cast into the deeper channel leading toward the city of New Haven. This area produces schoolie bass, occasional larger stripers, bluefish, weakfish, and snapper blues in season. To reach these West Haven fishing areas, take exit 44 off I-95, follow Route 122 west across the West River, take a left (a south turn, toward the water) onto First Street, and follow First to Beach Avenue, which butts into it near the corner at the West Haven Bars. Fish the shore and piers wherever possible along this area.

Up inside the harbor lies the Route 1 bridge. Take exit 49 off I-95, then follow Forbes Avenue back toward New Haven and over the Quinnipiac River. This is a popular and heavily fished access where anglers catch a few porgies during the summer, occasional winter flounder during the cold months, striped bass, and, later in summer into fall, snapper and adult bluefish. This bridge gets shoulder-to-shoulder, like opening day, when the bluefish are in and pushing bait up inside the Quinnipiac River. This portion of the harbor is lined with oil tanks and docks, making it a less-than-beautiful waterfront. The bottom is fairly barren, though it is loaded with worms and bivalves, which cannot be harvested due to the pollution levels in this area.

At the mouth of New Haven Harbor on the eastern side lies Lighthouse Park, a public access with deeper, more productive waters within an easy cast of shore. Take exit 50 off I-95, head east, pick up Townshend Avenue, follow it toward the Sound, take a right (west) onto Lighthouse Road, and follow to the park at its end.

Lighthouse Point Park to the outflow of Morris Creek's confluence with the Sound creates rip lines during tide changes that attract striped bass, weakfish, and bluefish when they are present in the area. Blackfish, porgies, and occasional flounder are caught from this location. Years back, while doing marine creel survey work at the park, I saw an angler using a 16-ounce beer can wrapped with monofilament line catch the largest American eel I've ever seen from the shore on the harbor side of this point. That eel was easily 5 feet long and 10 pounds!

Morris Creek is a fairly productive and popular snapper bluefish spot that also draws striped bass (mostly schoolies) and chopper blues to within casting distance of the beach. A boat launch at the park provides a needed boat access point in this part of the state. This launch, with room for 60 cars, is owned and operated by the city of New Haven, which collects fees on weekends and holidays.

This Lighthouse Point Launch provides a good site from which anglers with smaller craft can reach the three breakwalls that protect the mouth of this port. Anglers catch blackfish, striped bass, bluefish, porgies, and weakfish right along the rocks of these offshore rock structures. Fluke and winter flounder are taken by drifting the cleaner water and channels in between and leading up into the shoal waters around the harbor. In late summer the occasional false albacore and, more rarely, bonito—and during very hot summers, Spanish mackerel—have been caught from the waters around the breakwalls and out into the Sound, toward Townshend Ledge and Branford Reef farther to the east.

During the late 1990s and early in the new millennium, the New Haven/Milford/Branford area has consistently produced catches of weakfish; some anglers have even begun to target this species for the first time since they functionally disappeared from Connecticut waters during the late 1970s. Most weakfish are caught incidentally while fishing for schoolie stripers. Those who target these elusive and hard-to-catch fish, however are taking them on jigs tipped with some sort of fish; soft plastic lures such as Fin-S fish, Salt Shakers, and Shad Bodies; and plastic worms. The fake worms are fished "Texas style"—as in the technique used by largemouth bass fishermen, slip sinkers get them down—in shallow areas where these light rigs can easily reach the bottom. Simply stick the hook down the nose and out the belly of the worm about half an inch from the nose, then turn the hook 180 degrees and push it back up from the belly through the entire body so the barb barely breaks the surface: You have a Texas-rigged worm. Run an appropriate-sized slip sinker—anything from a quarter ounce on up is sufficient for most shallow-water applications—to get it to the bottom. Run a larger slip sinker ahead of a swivel tied a foot or two in front of the worm and you are "Carolina rigging"—another freshwater method that has many effective marine-fishing applications.

Many anglers launching boats at Lighthouse Point run east to fish the East Haven River or Farm River mouth, as well as nearby rocky structure such as Stony Island, East Indies Rocks, Cow and Calf, Gull Rocks, and Five Foot Rocks. All are fish-holding rocky structure, compliments of the glaciers, that lead into the maze of rocky ledges and islands that string off in an easterly direction toward the Thimble Islands.

BRANFORD

Shore-fishing access is very limited in this part of the state. Perhaps the most popular and fish-producing shore-based fishing spot is the pier at Branford Point. Boaters can launch at the Branford State Launch, a short distance away. The best path to the harbor is from exit 53 off I-95. Pick up Route 142, turn left onto Stannard Avenue, then right (south) onto Harbor Street, and follow it to the end at Branford Point Pier.

The Branford River channel swings to within an easy cast of the pier, making it a top-notch striper producer, particularly for those who fish the night shift. Historically this is a place that gives up some 30-pound-plus stripers every year to anglers casting live menhaden, hickory shad, or chunk baits such as menhaden or mackerel. Live eels and sandworms have also taken their share of big bass from this popular spot.

In the fall, when bluefish push peanut bunker and sometimes adult bunker up inside Branford River, fishing can be absolutely crazy: It's so narrow that the condensed schools of fish are reached with relative ease from shore or boat. When fish are abundant in the area, poppers, shallow-running swimmers, Slug-Gos, and cranking jigs (with Twister or Shad Bodies) will take their share of fish. When bass are present, soft plastics do well; when tackle-wrecking blues are in the river, hard baits and metal lures are most practical, though soft plastics will occasionally take fish when they aren't hitting hard lures or spoons very well.

Branford River State Launch lies just around the bend from Branford Point and can be reached from exit 53 off I-95. Take Route 142, then head left onto Stannard Avenue to Goodsell Point Road and the launch site. This is a small, 50-car launch in a heavily used area. On weekends from late spring through fall this place fills to capacity very quickly on all except very foul-weather days. In fact, it gets enough use that boaters seem to come in morning and afternoon shifts. It's difficult to find a spot to park most of the season, so hard-core anglers usually get to the launch in the dark. It's a very steep launch that is extremely shallow at low tide, which limits use by anglers fishing from larger trailerable boats to dropping and picking up when the tide is halfway on either side of the flood.

Branford Launch provides boat anglers a short run to Townshend Ledge, Branford Reef, Browns Reef, and the Thimble Islands—all very productive bluefish and bass grounds during the season. Anglers can employ any bait- or deep-fishing techniques around these reefs and expect to catch fish when they are present. Since the species' recovery, summer porgy fishing has been excellent off all these reefs and the many smaller reefs and rock piles in this area.

Townshend Ledge, Branford Reef, and Browns Reef are all top-notch blackfish destinations during the spring and fall runs. Fiddler crabs are the preferred blackfish bait, though green crabs are the most readily available and found in most bait shops. During the blackfish season, shop owners may run out of crabs, so it may be wise to reserve a supply or call around prior to fishing in order to be sure crabs or some other effective blackfish bait is available.

Connecticut regulations protect blackfish during their spawning season from May 1 through June 15, so the best of the spring blackfishing is missed during all except the warmest springs. During the fall run, many boats set up over these reefs and drop fiddler or green crabs right beside drop-offs, as well as any structure that shows above water or on a depth finder screen, on the downtide side of reefs. A few feet can make the difference in catching or not catching blackfish, so be prepared to pull up or let out anchor line in order to get the boat right on top of structure. When you're fishing in a good spot and set up properly, it can be easy to catch a limit of hard-fighting, great-eating blackfish (tautog).

To the east of Branford, off the string of islands extending south and east from Indian Neck, lies a spit of shallow water that runs from Sumac Island to the Negro Heads, which break the water at low tide. This shallow bar is a great place to drag tube and worm rigs, or to troll with shallow-running plugs and spreader rigs for bass and bluefish. It's also one of the spots that produces some of those weakfish in late summer or early fall.

The Thimble Islands, located near the quaint town of Stony Creek, are part of the glacial structure left behind after waters flooded the basin of Long Island Sound. These islands are primarily ledge that juts above sea level, with channels ranging from 8 to nearly 40 feet deep in between. The islands are a nightmare to run a boat through after dark, because there are so many "dry spots" at low tide. Sportfishermen who learn to navigate this maze of structure—including Commander Rocks, which lie along the outer edge of the Thimble Islands—will have invested their time wisely, because the Thimbles always hold rock-loving striped bass, blackfish, weakfish, and porgies. Both winter and summer flounder can be caught in the channels between the ledges and islands.

There is even a small local fishery for sharks off the outer edge of the Thimble Islands. Here knowledgeable anglers chum for and actually catch sand sharks, along with the occasional brown and small blue sharks that wander into Long Island Sound during the heat of summer. "Sharking" in the Thimble Islands has been a little-known fishery among local anglers for a couple of decades.

East of Branford, in the town of Guilford, lies the East River State Launch, located on east bank of the East River on the Madison town line. Take exit 59 on the east side of the river, follow Route 1 to Neck Road, and continue on Neck Road to the launch site at its end. This is another small launch with room for 25 cars, so get there early on the weekends. East River Launch provides the shortest hop to fish prime nearshore destinations such as Charles Reef, Indian Reef, and Madison Reef— a string of reefs and high spots running from Sachem Head to Tunxis Island, offshore and west of Hammonassett Beach.

Lying 3 or 4 miles off the coastline from Guilford are Kimberly Reef, Falkner Island, and, to the west, a bony spot

In Middlesex County off Madison lies Falkner Island, nearly a third of the way across the Sound. It and nearby Goose Island create terrific fishing grounds for those who have boats to get there. Striped bass, bluefish, weakfish, blackfish, scup, and fluke can all be targeted and caught in this area.

called Goose Island. The shoals around Falkner and Goose Islands provide a rocky, tide-swept shoal coming out of deep, mid-Sound waters that produces some of the best and biggest striped bass, bluefish, weakfish, blackfish, and small tuna that are taken in the waters off Middlesex County every season.

These islands also hold large concentrations of scup, which are very popular fish in this part of the state. The deeper waters around Falkner Island are home to some of the largest "humpbacks" caught in the state every season. The shoals between these islands and the expansive 20- to 40-foot-deep shoals to the west of Goose Island are also excellent areas over which to drift for summer flounder. The close proximity to the 90-foot depths of the open mid-Sound waters makes this an ideal location to catch a doormat fluke.

To the east of Falkner Island lies Kimberly Reef, a popular bluefish, striped bass, and porgy destination that is taken over by blackfish enthusiasts every fall. Anglers anchor up tight to the steep 30- to 40-foot drop-offs around this reef, lowering fiddler or green crabs down along the structure to the tautog that stack up in this spot every fall. Kimberly Reef is one of the premier blackfish destinations in this part of the state, with Falkner Island and Goose Island attracting good numbers of anglers seeking this species as well.

All summer and fall, anglers fishing with live eels, live menhaden, live hickory shad, and other prime bass baits can be seen running out to the Falkner Island area in the hope of landing some of the monster stripers that spend the season around this prime bit of offshore structure.

Fishermen launching in Guilford's East River, at Holiday Dock in Clinton Harbor, or out of Westbrook often run 4 to 5 miles due south of Westbrook Harbor and the Menunketesuch River to fish for bass, blues, porgies, and blackfish off Six Mile Reef. This is one of the area's most productive summer bluefish spots (along with Kimberly Reef). Fishermen trolling wire line bucktails, multiple-hook spreader rigs, or drifting the reefs with baited drail rigs, rigged squid, or live eels on three-way rigs do very well especially after dark. A few anglers are also using wire line or lead-core line to sink chunk baits or rigged squid down deep from a boat anchored uptide from the reefs. Occasionally bass and blues come up to the surface to feed—especially later in summer, when fish throughout the region seem to go on evening blitzes around all the major reefs and rip lines as the sun sets.

THE WHARVES TO HAMMONASSETT BEACH

Shore-based anglers are at a loss for public access areas in this part of the state. A few fish with limited success off the breakwalls at the mouth of the East River in Guilford. Some fish for snapper blues, occasional chopper blues, school bass, and (during winter) winter flounder from the town dock in Clinton Harbor. The best shore-fishing destinations in this part of the state are found in three locations along the rocks in the town of Madison.

East and West Wharves are two public fishing piers that both produce some decent shore-based catches during the course of an angling season. Take exit 61 off I-95, follow Route 79 south toward the Sound, take a right (west) onto Route 1, and make a quick left (south) onto Island Avenue. At the end, where it T's, head west to West Wharf or east along the water to East Wharf. The wharves are a little over a mile apart.

Most of the action from these rocky stretches comes from bass and bluefish in season or snapper blues later in summer. In spring and fall blackfish can be caught off the rocks, while porgies are omnipresent throughout the season. The area used to produce winter flounder, but not so much anymore. Fluke are occasionally caught here, though primarily from drifting boats. East Wharf, located inshore from Tunxis Island, is a place from which eel tossers and anglers fishing chunk baits through the night and into the hours around dawn often hook and land large striped bass, plus blues when they're present.

To the east is 2 mile long Hammonassett State Park—the largest public beach in the state of Connecticut. This popular state park has its own exit—exit 62 off I-95—that shunts traffic straight into the park; simply follow the signs. Hammonassett Beach is open to fishing during the off season and off hours, when the beach is not open to swimming. When the beach is being used during the summer season, anglers can fish from the jetties located at its eastern and western edges.

The west jetty at Hammonassett produced the only documented 20-pound-plus bluefish taken from the Connecticut surf during the years I was in charge of the Connecticut Marine Recreational Fisheries Program. One of the creel census people weighed a 22-pound monster taken at this spot. On another occasion I was personally working the beach doing fall interviews with surf fishermen. A school of menhaden passed by, blotting out the bottom with tightly packed fish being pushed up into the surf break by marauding blues. As I spoke to one fellow who had a pair of 13- to 15-pound choppers in the sand, he caught a fish that tipped the scales at 17 pounds!

Big aggressive bluefish are nothing new for this state park, which is a natural magnet for menhaden when they are in the area. Bunker frequently move into Clinton Harbor, then drop out of the harbor, swing around Meigs Point and along the beach with changing tides. More than once over the years, when bluefish were feeding on menhaden they had trapped in the surf break along Hammonassett Beach, swimmers were bitten. One time in the mid-1980s, when bluefish had filled the ecological void left after striped bass had been fished to oblivion, two women and a young boy were bitten very severely when they decided to swim with the fish like Cousteau. One of the swimmers required more than 100 stitches to close the gaping wounds left by what had to be some very large bluefish.

The moral of this story is: Don't ever be stupid enough to swim in a school of bunker (menhaden) especially not in fall, when they are probably being fed on by other frenzied bluefish.

Consistently, the most productive fishing to be found at this public state park is off Meigs Point Jetty, located at the eastern end of Hammonassett Point. The jetty and reef off its tip provide solid structure that attracts everything that swims. Anglers fishing both from shore and from boats off the reef consistently catch striped bass, bluefish, porgies, blackfish, snapper blues, weakfish, and even a bonito or false albacore in season. Of course the usual array of trash fish—cunners, searobin, skate, and sand sharks—are also a normal part of the catch. Unfortunately, at times they're most of the catch.

The beach itself is a great place to drift for fluke from a boat. After the beach is closed, or early in the morning before beachgoers arrive, anglers are also able to catch fluke by casting baited bucktails or live mummichogs into sandy areas adjacent to the jetty. Typically fluke will be in closer to the beach around the top of the tide, so look for action to be best during the two hours or so around high tide, when fluke are most likely to be in close to the surf break feeding.

Meigs Point Jetty, at the eastern end of Hammonassett State Park. Hammonassett Beach is a good fishing area and Meigs Point, which sticks off the end of the Clinton Harbor area, is a prime fishing spot that produces literally everything. It is perhaps the best shore-based fishing spot in Middlesex County.

The best single day of bluefishing this old rod-bender has experienced took place from a boat to the east of Meigs Point. The tide was high and dropping. We had been catching bluefish all day by locating menhaden schools, snagging a bait and letting it run, or casting poppers or plugs into the fray. In Clinton Harbor we found a huge school of menhaden that had been pushed into the shallows of the harbor along the eastern edge of Hammonassett Point—an area worth casting to from the shore when the tide is in at dawn or dusk.

Not to sound like an old fisherman's tale, but the water was boiling and off-colored by a combination of stirred-up sediments and menhaden blood. Its surface was slick with bunker oil. The air was filled with the pungent, fishy scent of bunker oil, blood and slime.

The blues that had this hapless school of bait cornered were very big choppers. Most of the fish we caught and released that afternoon were over 10 pounds, with the largest a full-fledged bunker nipper that tipped the Chatillion scales at just past the 17-pound mark!

The trip took place in September during what was literally the "calm following the storm"—a bright, sunny, mild day after the terrible destruction of Hurricane Gloria. Work was canceled that day, because the power was out. Rather than go home and rake leaves, three of us decided to go fishing for a few hours to see how the storm would affect our luck.

From the time we reached the Sound in front of Westbrook Harbor, we found and caught bluefish everywhere. Initially the blues were smaller, so we kept looking for new schools, and catching fish, until we located a pod of larger choppers. Before we reached Clinton Harbor, three of us had caught and released about 70 blues ranging from 4 up to about 8 pounds. For about three hours around the high tide, in that shallow pocket along Hammonassett Point, we lost track of the catch-and-release "body count" at somewhere around 135—and we easily took 10 apiece after we stopped counting. An incredible day of fishing, period.

Our method was basic live-lining. With large treble hooks on a short wire leader we would approach a school of bait, cast into the fray, snag a menhaden, and let it swim. Within seconds or, at worst, minutes, a bluefish would be chomping our baits to pieces. Then the hook was set and the fight was on.

We were using light spinning gear, making for maximum sport with every fish. Because we were setting the hook immediately upon a strike, only one or two of the blues we caught were gut-hooked badly enough that they couldn't be released to fight again.

The fact is, this exact set of circumstances may never occur again in my lifetime. Still, every summer you will find bluefish and striped bass cornering bait in the pockets around Meigs Point or the West Jetty at Hammonassett, or along the shoreline heading in toward Clinton Harbor. When bait is abundant, blues often push their prey well up inside the harbor; they have been observed smacking into the bottoms of moored boats in the marinas that line the Hammonassett River as it winds behind the park and away from the Sound.

Nearby to the east, Duck Island, Kelsey Point (Clinton Harbor) Breakwall, Menunketesuck Island off its namesake river, and the port of Westbrook provide what little solid offshore striper-holding structure there is on this stretch of coastline. The white ribbon of Hammonassett Beach is not only the best shore-based fishing access in Middlesex County but also a landmark that many boat anglers key in on. The waters nearby consistently hold fish of all species and are worth exploring anytime of the season—but particularly in late summer and fall, when bluefish abound and the big bass begin moving westward through the Sound toward their wintering and spawning grounds in the Hudson River.

4

Eastern Connecticut (New London County)

THE CONNECTICUT RIVER AND VICINITY

The Connecticut River is the largest in New England. It originates in the Connecticut Lakes region of northern Vermont, just a few miles from the Canadian border. From there it flows southward to the Long Island Sound, bisecting both Massachusetts and Connecticut in the process. Its tremendous freshwater flow is a major factor in shaping not only the state's shoreline, but eastern Long Island Sound as well. Its fresh water, when combined with the inflows of other large rivers such as the Housatonic, Thames, Quinnipiac, and Pawcatuck—not to mention smaller flowages including the Saugatuck River, East River, Eight Mile River, and others—actually reduces the salinity of the Sound by a few parts per thousand from ocean levels.

On a map or from a plane, it's possible to see how the Connecticut River cuts its way across Long Island Sound, through Plum Gut, near Gardners Island. A chart readily demonstrates how it digs out the bottom past Montauk Point, ultimately gouging a notch in the continental shelf known as Block Island Canyon. During the 500-year floods of 1992, while I was doing survey work from a small plane, the tremendous freshet caused by this benchmark flood could be seen as a rippled, coffee-colored river of surface water flowing over the top of the denser salt waters of the Sound. It bore straight across Long Island Sound to Plum Gut before its influence was lost in the green waters of the Atlantic.

This flood was so strong that it carried freshwater species out of many rivers to their doom in the saltwater environment. A few days after this tremendous flood, sample seine nets I pulled near the mouth of the Thames River (which were intended to catch and identify juvenile shad stocked as fertilized eggs that spring in the Quinebaug River) yielded bluegills (*Lepomis macrochirus*); a nearby salt creek (Alewife Cove, Waterford) held small schools of lost and dying carp that had also been washed out into the Sound in the pockets of fresh water that were fast dissipating.

The Connecticut River has long been considered the state's best all-around fishery resource. Its upper reaches hold numerous species of freshwater and anadromous fish, including salmon, shad, herring, pike, walleye, largemouth bass, smallmouth bass, perch (white and yellow), channel catfish, white catfish, sturgeon, and even bowfin.

Striped bass frequent the lower reaches of the river all summer long, along with hickory shad, bluefish, blue crabs, occasional weakfish, winter flounder, and fluke (summer flounder). There are even some porgies around the railroad and I-95 abutments in summer when freshwater inflows are minimal.

Prior to the crash of winter flounder populations in Connecticut during the late 1970s and early 1980s, anglers fished successfully for this species from the causeway across South Cove; at the seawall and adjacent riverbanks; near Dock and Dine Restaurant at the end of Main Street in Saybrook; and from the Saybrook Town Dock, located on the Sound to the west of the river's mouth. Since the species has all but disappeared along much of the Connecticut coastline, these spots receive little targeted angler effort for winter flounder, but all remain good-to-excellent sites from which to catch striped bass, adult and snapper bluefish, occasional weakfish, fluke, and scup.

To get to these places, take exit 66 or 67 off I-95, pick up Route 1, turn south onto Route 154, and follow it around in a big loop back to Route 1. The fishing access points are located wherever the road runs close to the water. From the west you can fish for snapper blues, school bass, or blue crabs where Route 1 crosses over Oyster River, or where Route 154 crosses the tide creek near Harveys

An angler casts toward some breaking striped bass at the mouth of South Cove, Saybrook, with the Connecticut River Lighthouse in the background.

Beach. Route 154 passes by the Town Dock and Beach near Guardhouse Point, near the Saybrook Lighthouse. It passes over the causeway as it swings north along the river past Fenwick (where Katherine Hepburn lives.) The Dock and Dine and access points in that area are found where the road turns north and back up the main drag through Old Saybrook.

During the 1980s, the Department of Environmental Protection (DEP) built a 1,000-foot-long fishing pier and observation walkway that follows the shoreline from Marine District

Headquarters in Lyme on under the railroad trestle, and a few hundred feet into the mouth of the Lieutenant River. Take exit 70 off I-95, pick up Route 156 heading south (toward the Sound) from the highway, turn right onto Ferry Road, and follow the signs to the DEP's Marine District Headquarters; the fishing access pier and ample parking are at the end. Anglers fish for white perch, school stripers, and blue crabs off the bridge where Route 156 crosses the Lieutenant River just beyond Ferry Road. There's a second small access point on the Lieutenant River in the short stretch of Route 1 between the east- and westbound exit 70s, which are separated by about a mile. This place provides the same type of action: limited, seasonal fishing for snapper blues, school stripers, white perch, and blue crabs. Rarely, sea-run brown trout are caught in the lower Lieutenant River; these are "drop-down" trout from stockings upstream.

The public fishing pier at Marine Headquarters provides one of the better and more productive shore-based angler access points in this part of the state. This site is handicapped friendly—one of the few such spots that actually produces fish of many species on a regular basis throughout the fishing year. The corner of the pier south of the railroad bridge is a great spot for striped bass in spring. White perch and hickory shad are also present during spring and summer. Bluefish, both adult and snappers, are caught off the walkway. Resourceful anglers who work at it may also be able to take a fluke from time to time, but they are not very common here. Porgies and blackfish can be caught by casting the appropriate baits to the railroad bridge abutments from the dock. The hole to the north of the bridge also holds some tomcod during the cold-weather fishing months, along with behemoth bass in season.

This spot is also an excellent blue crabbing destination when this species is active during summer and early fall. Crabbers can toss bait on strings and haul the crabs to the net, set crab traps, or net crabs off the pilings.

Boat anglers will find two excellent launch sites on either side of the lower river in Old Saybrook and Old Lyme. The Connecticut River State Launch located under the I-95 bridge in Saybrook is the deeper of the two, but may cause problems for some larger boats at dead low tide. Access is easy from I-95. Take Route 9 north off I-95 on the west side of the Connecticut River. Off the exit ramp turn right; the road passes under the bridge about a mile down. The launch is under the bridge. There is ample parking for 75 trailers, but like all the state launch sites it fills up quickly during summer.

The Great Island State Launch, on the east side of the river in Old Lyme, is a mid- to high-tide launch, especially under moon-tide conditions. It can be reached by taking exit 70 off I-95. Head south on Route 156 past Ferry Road and the Marine Headquarters to the BOAT LAUNCH sign at Smith Neck Road; the launch is at the end. This is a smaller access area with parking for 35 trailers. Both launch areas provide good access to the lower Connecticut River, with the Great Island Launch being closer to the good fishing areas at the river mouth and shortest run to the Sound.

Fishermen launching in Saybrook will have a short no-wake zone to go through, which ends at the railroad bridge. Great Island is best suited to small craft and trailerable boats under 20 feet. Low tide can pose problems for all but the shallowest-draft boats.

Anglers who don't mind walking, or those with a small boat or kayak, can walk from Old Shore Road at White Sands Beach to the end of Griswold Point, where the Blackhall River tide creek empties into the Connecticut River on its eastern edge.

At Griswold Point, a deep hole—about 20 feet—has been carved out of the shallow bottom sediments by the strong tidal currents. It is tucked up against the muddy walls of Great Island. This hole is one of those spots that always hold fish. Flounder, fluke, bass, blues, and (when they're in the area) weakfish will sit in the relatively dark depths, sucking up the bait pulled out of the tide creeks with the ebbing tide. It is an easy spot to reach by boat, and a long cast from shore. Shore-based anglers, however, have the relatively strong fish-attracting current that runs around Griswold Point sandbar with the changing tides to work with plugs or bait. Anglers with canoes and kayaks often paddle down along Great Island, pull the canoe up onto dry land, and walk to the deep hole to fish with flies or light spinning gear with great success. Another option is to go out along the river and paddle to the Wood Lot, a clump of trees along the middle of the western edge of Great Island, and fish the rocks at high tide. During the spring and fall striper runs this is one of the hottest shallow-water fishing zones anywhere in the state. The same area also draws bluefish during summer and fall.

Fishermen using boats have continued to experience fair-to-moderate success in catching winter flounder off the mouth of the Connecticut River from late spring into early summer, despite low population levels throughout the region.

As freshwater flows stabilize and slow after spring flooding and snowmelt to the north, winter flounder move into the mouth of the Connecticut River, where they concentrate and are harvested by anglers fishing the shallow waters from the breakwall to Griswold Point. A few fish are taken outside the river mouth to Long Sand Shoal and on either side of the break-walls, where back eddies attract and hold fish.

The majority are taken by anglers who set chum pots and concentrate their efforts near the visible line created where dirty, often brownish fresh water meets the more green and clear salt water during the incoming tide. This line moves in the direction of the prevailing tides, so the best way to fish is to drift over it, or anchor nearby and let out anchor line to stay near the edge. Flatfish generally concentrate on the ocean side of this line. Anglers who fish off an anchor are wise to set up on the clear saltwater side of this line. When winds and tides are right, it's possible to catch flatfish by repeatedly drifting spreader rigs or single-hook high/low rigs decorated with bright yellow, orange, or chartreuse beads and baited with sandworm pieces. There are times when winter flounder can be caught successfully in less than 10 feet of water, making this a very effective technique when conditions are right. Otherwise it's most productive to anchor somewhere within a few hundred yards to the east of the eastern or "outer" breakwall and set a chum pot.

At best, this fishing is a far cry from the catches that were historically made here and along most of the southern New England coastline. At present, anglers brag when they catch an eight-fish limit of 12-inch flatfish—a catch that wouldn't have even prompted old-time flounder fishermen to launch their boats 25 to 35 years ago. No one knows why winter flounder have not responded as positively to the current strict angling regulations and commercial quotas that have been put in place to protect and (hopefully) rebuild these beleaguered stocks. This species was destroyed by overharvest, primarily from commercial trawlers that harvested these fish inshore, right off the beaches, from the time they first began moving around after their spawning activities in March and on through the summer, when they retreated to the cooler, deeper waters of Long and Block Island Sounds.

Constant, nearly year-round fishing pressure during the 1970s and 1980s depleted stocks. I believe that warming water temperatures have not been conducive to spawning of these cold-loving fish. In addition, huge increases in populations of predatory species such as seals, cormorants, and striped bass—which feed heavily on winter flounder juveniles as well as adults—have combined to hold winter flounder production and recruitment to a minimum. The result has been little or no improvement in winter flounder populations in most areas throughout the region.

The strong conservation measures that have helped rebuild popul tions of striped bass, fluke, and scup simply have not worked in favor of winter flounder in southern New England. There have been a few isolated areas where flatfish numbers have increased noticeably over the near-zero levels of a few years ago. The mouth of the Connecticut River is one of these minor flounder-producing spots. The other notable areas are Niantic Bay a few miles to the east and, more recently, Clinton Harbor to the west.

The Connecticut River and vicinity provides some of the best spring striper fishing in the region between mid-April and June, when striped bass that are migrating from the Hudson River provide some excellent fishing as far upriver as a boat can travel.

When alewives, blueback herring, and American shad are running up the Connecticut River to spawn, they draw some huge stripers right to base of and even over the Enfield Dam. Sometime between late April and the end of May every spring, a fabulous shore-based and boat fishery develops in the rapids and runs below the Enfield Dam and points downriver.

As of spring 2002, a total prohibition on the taking of alewives and blueback herring for any purpose in Connecticut waters was in place. This move effectively ended the live herring fishery for big bass that once developed each spring in Connecticut's major coastal rivers with the arrival of these clupeid species.

Nothing beats using a live "buckey" (the local name for alewives and blueback herring) as a live bait to catch jumbo striped bass—anywhere. Anglers can still use frozen baits such as mackerel or menhaden, which are not quite as effective. Some anglers have talked of tossed jumbo, pike-sized shiners in lieu of herring, an idea that has some merit. Otherwise, in order to stay legal, throw large, shallow-running swimming plugs such as Yozuri Swimmers, Mambo Minnows (in blue or Gray Ghost colors), or big soft plastics, such as Fin-S fish or Slug-Gos, in the 10- and 9-inch sizes, respectively. All these 7- to 10-inch-long artificials are proven striper catchers when herring are running.

Striped bass can be caught anywhere along the river during the spring run and in the lower half in fall. Anglers fishing for largemouth and smallmouth bass during spring and fall often take school stripers accidentally. Look for the stripers to collect around any hard structure or inflowing creeks, as they would along the coast. Places such as South Cove, Essex, and Hamburg Cove are notable striper hot spots during the spring striper runs.

The best striper action will be found from Essex to the mouth and for a mile or so below the Enfield Rapids during the spring run.

Areas of the lower river around Great Island, the Lieutenant River, North and South Cove on the west side as well as the abutments from the two bridges that cross the lower river in Lyme, and the breakwalls all provide excellent striper-holding structure.

Great Island is the most popular fishing spot during the spring schoolie fishing season, which usually revs up in late April or early May. This is an area that is good fishing anytime, but best on the ebb tide. In the past friends and I have found that an hour or two of fishing the ebb tide, especially under low-light conditions of dawn or dusk, is usually two to five times more productive than fishing an entire flood tide.

The waters off Great Island are shallow—too shallow for larger boats at dead low tide. But around the top of the tide and first three hours or so of the ebb, the entire side of the river from Lieutenant River to Griswold Point comes alive with school bass, which may be joined by bluefish later in spring and on into summer and fall.

A wise routine to follow is to fish the end of the flood up close to the banks and up inside the coves and Lieutenant River. As the tide turns, look for rip lines to set up where creeks empty into the river from Great Island. Rock piles from old haul seine sites create hot spots during the tide, but may also eat a prop or lower unit, so refer to a chart and keep your eyes peeled for ripples and riffles that indicate the presence of these dangerous but productive striper holding structures.

Typically schoolies will feed their way downriver along the island with the tide. If the action levels slow or stop in one area, begin searching downstream with the tide. When water levels are up, fish close to the bank. As the tide drops, the bass—especially the larger fish—will be drawn out to the deep channel, which swings out toward the Saybrook side of the river as you move toward the river mouth, where the channel passes between the breakwalls on the western side of the river mouth.

In spring, a great day's fishing can be planned around a combo winter flounder/striper outing. To be successful, an accurate tide chart is a must. Plan the trip when high tide falls around 4 to 5 P.M.

Start off fishing for winter flounder around noon as the flood tide first begins to push the saltwater/freshwater line upriver. Set up on an anchor with a chum pot along the east breakwall or drift around the edge of the green water for best chance of taking a few flatfish.

At high slack tide, pick up the flatfish spreaders and head upriver to Great Island for the turn of the tide and first few hours of the ebb tide, as the sun sets. Before the winter flounder were fished out, we used to easily take dozen-pound-plus flounder and top the day off with a catch-and-release bonanza on schoolie bass up to about 12 pounds. Our catch could total 50 fish or more, for two skilled anglers, in a couple of hours when conditions were right.

At present, count your lucky stars if you take a limit or even half a limit of winter flounder, though the bass are usually cooperative throughout spring. There is always a chance to hook into a jumbo striper on the flats, especially later in spring, when the herring chasers drop out of the upper river and the big breeders from the Hudson and Chesapeake Bay are moving through the area on their northward migration.

One common problem can be heavy, flooding rains that take place in spring. A couple of inches of rain throughout the region will turn the river brown, clog it with debris, pick up flow rates, and literally blow both bass and flatfish out into the Sound, killing all fishing for a few days until conditions stabilize.

As the summer season arrives, striper abundance will thin down to a steady summertime level of schoolies. These remain in the lower river, providing the most consistent fishing early and late in the day or after dark. Winter flounder will become very scarce, but will be replaced by fluke (summer flounder) by the end of May or early June, depending on water temperatures and river flows.

Fluke fishing is usually excellent off the Connecticut River's mouth anywhere from North Cove out to Long Sand Shoal, with the lower river in front of the inflowing coves and tide creeks being the prime spots. The Connecticut River produces some of the larger "doormats" reported in the eastern half of the Connecticut coastline each summer. The abundance of food, including juvenile herring and menhaden, is the draw.

Samantha (the dog) asks my wife Karen how she caught that nice fluke. Populations are on the increase, making it relatively easy for even a skilled dog to take a fluke here and there.

The best, most consistent fishing in this area is for larger striped bass, once the big fish leave the river and summertime temperature regimes take over. These fish will be found around the major reefs within 5 miles on either side of the river mouth or around Long Sand Shoal, which runs for a couple of miles parallel to the coastline and about 2 miles outside the river mouth. Deeper holes and pockets in the shoal are spots to key in on when jigging, trolling, drifting live eels or baits for big striped bass.

To the east, within a short boat run, lies Hatchett Reef—one of the state's premier big-bass-producing spots. Anglers cast plugs and drift eels or chunk baits from the rocky shore at Hatchett Point on out to the deep waters off the seaward side of Hatchett Reef, for about a mile off the shoreline. Hatchett Reef is a great all-around fishing spot and the first major piece of solid structure to the east of the river mouth.

The shoreline at Hatchett Point is privately owned, so shore access is limited. Any boat, however, can take a swing to the left on its way out of the Connecticut River, run to the first rocky point along the shore, and begin fishing from there out to the buoys that mark the rocky terminus of this highly productive fishing spot. Hatchett Reef always holds striped bass, bluefish, blackfish, porgies, and fluke in the sandy areas around the rocks. In late summer false albacore and bonito may swing through the area, but they don't usually hold in this particular spot.

To the west of the river mouth lies boulder-strewn Cornfield Point. Offshore from the point is a rocky reef known as the Chickens and Hens; it's a few hundred yards off the point itself. The point and reef, with its strong current-swept rocks, make for an excellent big-bass destination that is both a great surf-casting area from the rocks and a super place to fish from a boat. Unfortunately, depending on who owns the Cornfield Point Inn at any given time, shore access may not always be open to the angling public. The best time to fish from the rocks is between owners and after hours. Some owners have granted permission to locals to fish. There is ample parking in the lot at the inn, and it's a short but tricky walk over the boulders to the water.

The rock piles that create Cornfield Reef are among the top big-bass spots to fish from a boat in this area. The most productive method of catching large bass here—like everywhere else—is drifting or casting live eels, live hickory shad, or, when available, live menhaden (or chunk baits made of these fish or mackerel) into and around the visible and submerged structure. This is also a place where artificial lures such as swimming plugs, poppers, soft plastics like Fin-S fish, Slug-Gos, Shad Bodies, and squid imitations will do some damage on the big bass that hold on this spot through the season. Once the prop-eating rocks have been identified, it's a great-looking place to drag a tube and worm rig as well.

For a convenient bait and tackle stop near all these great places like "Rivers End Bait and Tackle" on Route 1, the way towards I-95 from Saybrook.

ROCKY NECK STATE PARK

Located off Route 156 in the town of East Lyme, Rocky Neck State Park provides the only state access to the coastline with available camping. Reservations are necessary well in advance of the summer season. Still, day-trippers can come and fish off the jetty at the park's west end or at the mouth of Bride Brook, which empties into the Sound under a railroad overpass.

This is primarily a swimming beach. Every so often, big stripers are caught off the mouth of Bride Brook in spring when they are chasing the alewives that run up the brook to spawn. Later in summer, when flows subside, the brook becomes a tidal creek and is a good place to catch snapper blues and crabs. Most of the remainder of the year, the long jetty—with relatively shallow water all around—is most productive around high tide. A smattering of fluke, porgies, and, after dark, bluefish and stripers are caught from the rocks. Rocky Neck has arguably the poorest fishing of all the coastal state parks east of New Haven, due primarily to the very shallow, sandy, essentially featureless habitat around it. Harkness Park to the east and Hammonassett State Park to the west are much better fishing areas.

5

Niantic Bay and Vicinity

Niantic Bay is one of the largest natural estuaries in Connecticut. Its gradually shoaling water, as one moves in from the Sound, with structure-lined shore, is a natural attractant for all species of fish. The bay and "Niantic River"—as the large embayment north of the constricting bridges is known— are fantastic fishing destinations for both shore and boat fishermen. I can only imagine how fishy this area would be if the construction of bridges and roads during the industrial revolution had not cut off the water circulation which caused rapid filling and sedimentation of the upper bay, particularly along the roads.

Unfortunately, like so much of the Connecticut coast, the shore-based access is very limited. Due to the extreme shoals of the upper bay, even if there were good shore access, most of it would not be worth casting a line into given the vast expanses of shallow water between shore and the channel, where most of the fish are located.

At the extreme upper end of Niantic River, where Latimer Brook enters the tide water, are two very limited shore-fishing spots. Take exit 75 off I-95 and head east on Route 1. Right there, at a place called the Old Mill, is the pool where Latimer Brook dumps into Niantic Bay.

This unique fishing hole is one of the better sea-run brown trout sites in the entire state. You can park in a nearby lot or at a wide pullover off the road and walk down to the water, where you can wade out to present lures, baits, or flies to sea-run browns or even stocked drop-down trout, depending on the season. You can also also take white perch. Essentially it's a sea-run brown trout place with a short window of time each year—from November through May—when the fish are around and likely to be caught.

Sea-run browns begin moving into their natal spawning streams (actually the streams where they were released as fingerlings) in fall when water temperatures begin to drop, normally during late October or early November. The fish remain in the upper bay from then through late March or early April, when rising water temperatures drive them back into the cooler waters of Long Island Sound.

During April and May, trout fishermen occasionally encounter drop-down stocked trout from the excellent put-and-take fishery of Latimer Brook. They are also driven out of the area by June most years.

The brook makes a U-turn and heads southward back under the Route 1 bridge a second time within a tenth of a mile of the Old Mill. This is called the "Golden Spur" by anglers and is an interesting fishing location. It historically yielded some of the largest sea-run browns ever caught in the state. Waters here are deep and salty, so tomcod, winter flounder, white perch, hickory shad, snapper bluefish, and even the occasional striped bass or weakfish happen by during the year.

Access is around the bridge, where most land is privately owned and closed to trespassers. Fishing from the bridge, though allowed, is foolhardy because of the volume of traffic that passes by at high speed only a few feet away from the rails. Though there is shore access to the Golden Spur, it is perhaps a better, certainly safer, small-boat fishing area.

Flounder can be caught on sandworms, which will also catch tomcod and white perch in early spring and late winter—late February through March—when they are present in abundance. During the summer, hickory shad will readily strike standard shad darts, flies tied to small spoons, or any flashy, brightly colored lure or fly less than 2 inches long. Stripers and weakfish will hit small jigs, swimming plugs, flies, and small soft plastics. This is not a place that is likely to produce much more than school stripers.

Sea-run trout will take small trout spoons, spinners, and swimming plugs such as Rapalas in the 2-inch or 3-inch size. Generally, the smaller 1- to 2-pound sea-runs are the fish that fall for artificials. Over the years the majority of sizable sea-runs—those over 4 pounds—have been caught using light spinning tackle and an unweighted hook, possibly floated off a tiny bobber but usually straight-lined, baited with the largest mummichog available. Dead mummies can be hooked through the lips and cast like a lure on a one-sixteenth- or one-eighth-ounce jighead.

Historically, the best method is to cast and retrieve the free-hooked mummies like small living lures. A few sea-runs have been caught incidentally on sandworms by anglers fishing for flounder, but the majority are taken on large, live mummichogs fished from ice-out through late March, with the fall period of late November through early January when ice forms being nearly as productive.

Unfortunately, the sea-run trout program—which hit its peak during the late 1960s and early 1970s—was dropped during the late 1970s when Atlantic salmon began returning to the Connecticut River. During the 2002 fishing season it has been resurrected via fingerling stockings, which will hopefully restore this once great trophy trout fishery.

On the way down Oswegatchie Road, south of Route 1 and a mile east of the Golden Spur, lies a small public access called Kiddie Beach. It's not much of a beach, nor much of a fishing spot, except during late winter or early spring, when winter flounder move up into its shallow waters to spawn. There is normally a window of time of perhaps a week when you can catch large winter flounder from the shallow, narrow cove. Other than that occasional school bass may be present during high tide during the peak of spring and fall fishing periods, and snapper bluefish show up in late summer. All the fisheries in this shallow-water area are best around high tide, when there is 4 to 6 feet of water in the depths of the small cove where Kiddie Beach is located.

The remainder of the "river" is pretty much private land, until you reach the bridges and road that separate the river from Niantic Bay proper. For this reason, most of the fishing above the bridges is done from boats. Anglers who don't have dock space on the bay can depart from the state launch on the Waterford side of the river.

In winter during good years, scallops and clams can be dug in the upper bay. Winter flounder are still present in the Niantic River, but in low numbers. During spring, summer, and fall, striped bass, bluefish, snapper blues, and hickory shad can be taken throughout the season. In recent years a few weakfish have been caught from the Niantic River in its upper reaches near Sandy Point and along the channel by anglers fishing for school bass and hickory shad.

The best action all summer in recent years has been coming from the huge schools of hickory shad that enter the river through the constriction and feed their way to the head of the bay during the incoming tide. They then drop back down, collecting in the basin above the bridges, where they are very vulnerable to anglers with light tackle and flies.

Some fishermen are after the hickory shad for the sport they provide on light tackle and fly rods. Others are catching them for use as live hook baits for big striped bass and as chunk baits for bass and bluefish.

The best shore-based fishing in Niantic Bay is the area known as "Between the Bridges." This is the narrow constriction created by engineers who built the railroad and road bridges across the bay back in the 1800s. Though the upper bay or river is shallow, with a 6- to 10-foot-deep channel snaking through it, the scouring action of tidal movements between the bridges cuts a 20-foot-deep channel that screams when tides are flushing out. The combination of strong currents, bridge and dock pilings creates a terrific fish-attracting-and-holding habitat that anglers can exploit.

Shore-based anglers can take exit 74 off I-95, head south on Route 161, then proceed east on Route 156. As you drive along the picturesque "Sand Bar" that approaches along the west side of the bay, with a gorgeous view of Niantic Bay and the river, look for a pull-off to the right that takes you under the bridge to ample parking and the *Blackhawk* headboat parking as well. You can exit your car and walk to various spots along the riprap of the bridge abutments and banks to fish. Many head out across the tracks to cast where the waters dump into Niantic Bay in a mass of swirling currents. Others work their way along the extensive but shallow beach. At times when the tide is in, striped bass, blues, weakfish (rarely), and even false albacore push bait against this beach, which was formed by the filling and laying of railroad tracks across the bay more than a century ago. Anglers catch winter flounder and fluke in this area along with the larger, more glorious predators.

Between the Bridges is one of the more productive shore fishing places for about everything found in Connecticut waters. It is a natural concentration point for bait, which in turn attracts predators. Back in the 1970s, when I first began writing about the fishing activity in eastern Connecticut, an angler who was a friend of Captain Ernie Shiller of the *Mijoy*—a headboat that moors on the east side of the channel—had special permission to fish from the *Mijoy* docks. Because he was literally the only one who had access to the point where the channel cuts the deepest in this productive area, he consistently made the reports from both nearby Hillyer's Bait and Tackle as well as those turned in by Captain Shiller. This gentle man, whose name I have forgotten, caught one of the few bona fide 60-pound stripers recorded in Connecticut waters, on a live eel one evening during the July big-bass run.

Last year fishermen working the rocks on the opposite side from the *Mijoy* accounted for many 20- to 40-pound bass, some fluke, loads of big blackfish up to 10 pounds (during the spring and fall runs), as well as bluefish, snapper blues, tons of hickory shad, and an occasional weakfish. The day that I completed the first draft of this book, a fisherman using a live hickory shad caught a 47-inch striper from Between the Bridges. The presence of hickory shad always draws some big bass into the area, which remain as long as the hickories are there to prey on.

Blackfish and porgies are a common catch around the pilings—which often cut off some of the larger fish that are hooked every season.

Between the Bridges is most productive from dusk through dawn, with most of the bigger bass taken each year falling prey to anglers casting live eels, menhaden, or hickory shad after dark.

On the eastern side of this cut are two headboats—the *Mijoy* and *Sunbeam Fleet*—along with a small fleet of charter boats, private docking, and one of the state's largest public launch sites, the Niantic Bay State Launch. On the west side of the cut is the *Blackhawk* headboat and a marina that rents boats as well as providing slips for the public. Farther west in Niantic itself are a host of marinas, each with private dock facilities and more small-boat charter captains for hire. In this area, ask for Captain Dan Woods, one of the more famous names in the Niantic fleet.

The headboats target their trips for fluke, striped bass, and bluefish, depending on the season. Early in the season the *Sunbeam* runs across to sample the great fluke fishing of Peconic Bay, Long Island. Later in the year, when fishing sets up locally, it plies the waters from Niantic Bay to the mouth of the Connecticut River for fluke.

The *Sunbeam*, *Blackhawk*, and *Mijoy* all switch over to striped bass and bluefish, primarily in the Race, when these larger gamefish are present in fishable numbers, starting sometime in late May or June. Essentially they fish for whatever is running strongest, with the emphasis on bluefish and bass from early summer through fall. Around Labor Day the *Sunbeam Express*—a 100-foot boat rigged for offshore overnight trips—takes weekly overnight fishing excursions to the tuna-fishing grounds along the continental shelf in places such as the Fishtails, Block Canyon, and the Dip.

The Niantic Bay State Launch provides anglers with trailerable boats access to some of the best fishing in eastern Connecticut waters. The launch is just beyond the pull-off for Between the Bridges. Simply cross the river, make the first left, follow the exit ramp to its end, make a quick left onto River Road and then a right, and follow the BOAT RAMP signs at the edge of the water. The launch is located inside the river on the east bank of the upper bay. Across the street is Hillyer's Bait and Tackle, a full-service bait-and-tackle shop within walking distance of the launch that has anything anglers will need for a day on the water.

Boat fishermen can literally start fishing as soon as they run under the railroad bridge. Given the heavy boat traffic and the fact that many shore-based anglers cast their lines here, however, it's a spot that should be left for rainy days, when you won't be interfering with other people running boats or fishing. It's only polite, when you are in a boat and have access literally to the entire bay, to stay away from places where shore-based anglers are fishing.

It's best to run to either side of the bay, being sure to scan for working birds or surface breaks, because fish may show up literally anywhere in the Niantic Bay area, especially in later summer and fall when stripers, bluefish, and false albacore begin pushing small bait, creating surface blitzes nearly every evening and occasionally throughout the day.

Anglers who like to cast can work the entire western side of the bay from McCooks Point, a small town access beach. The beach is closed to fishing except during the off season, but the rocky shoreline from the bluff provides decent angling opportunities—particularly during high water—to fishermen targeting porgies, blackfish, fluke, flounder, striped bass, and bluefish of all sizes from snappers on up. A large pound net set out in front of this area attracts many fish due not only to the abundance of smaller fish swimming in the net, but also to the fish released from the net when it's checked. It acts like a huge natural chum pot at certain times of the year, especially when menhaden are in the area.

Black Point, which looks like a huge upside-down thumb jutting out into Long Island Sound at the end of Niantic Bay's west side, is one of the premier fishing destinations in the entire region. Off the tip of the point is a 100-foot-deep hole that produces some of the largest fluke taken in the state every summer, as well as bluefish and huge striped bass. Later in summer and fall small tuna such as false albacore and bonito can also be taken from the rip lines that set up over the shoals in this area.

The bottom comes up fairly abruptly from the deep shoals to around 30 feet before reaching a shallow rocky shelf at the shoreline. The entire area is loaded with striped bass from May through fall, and bluefish beginning in late June. The shoal creates a fish-holding rip line that often produces those "after-work" surface blitzes from feeding blues and bass from late summer through fall.

The Patagansett River, with a complex estuary dotted with sand and rock islands, creates another excellent habitat where it meets Long Island Sound along the western side of Black Point. The result is an area that has every sort of structure and therefore holds every variety of gamefish throughout the year, including many of the largest striped bass and fluke logged into area tackle shops every season.

To the east lies Millstone Point. This area has had no shore-based access and limited boat-based fishing opportunities since September 11, 2001, for obvious reasons: No one is allowed anywhere near the intake canal to the Millstone Point Nuclear Power Plant, which was once a very productive fishing zone. Still, boats have been allowed to fish up into the warm-water discharge at the tip of Millstone Point. This hot-water discharge is, like all such outflows, a fish magnet. Because this one is located on Long Island Sound, close to

Millstone Point outflow, the warm-water discharge from the Millstone Point Nuclear Plant, is a magnet for fish. This area produces some great false albacore fishing every summer.

its mouth, it always seems to draw fish early and keep them late, possibly holding schools of bluefish, bass, occasionally even false albacore well into winter, until a shutdown allows cold-water intrusion—which unfortunately turns all but the bass into lobster food.

Over the years this spot has attracted numerous tropical species including queen angelfish, Spanish mackerel, and even tarpon up to 100 pounds during some of those really warm summers in the 1980s. Of course it's better known as a hot spot (literally and figuratively) for blues, bass, and, later in summer and fall, bonito, false albacore, and Spanish mackerel. Some years these species are held in the warm-water outflow, where food is abundant and temps remain their liking well past the point where they can survive in the ambient waters outside. I've seen false albacore stacked like cordwood in this discharge as late as December during an exceptionally warm fall, but they were not hitting very well, and we could not claim a catch during December.

Earlier that summer the false albies that filled the discharge plume would turn on at dark and readily whack swimming jigs such as Shad Bodies on jigs, Salt Shakers, Slug-Gos, swimming plugs, and spoons. Chrome-colored Mambo Minnows are also, for some reason, very productive false albacore lures. Anglers throw cast nets from their boats or shore into the huge schools of bait in the calm spots. The bait would then be used as chum and hook baits. All that needed to be done was to stick one on a hook, toss it into the discharge outflow, and *bam*, fish on—much more pro-

John Hillyer holds up a 3-pound fluke, typical for the Niantic Bay area.

ductive than any artificial lure. The baitfishermen were taking fish every cast, while us lure casters often cast for half an hour or more between hookups during daylight hours. However, when the sunset blitzes began, hookups came every third cast or so.

The problem was, the fish were difficult to keep on, because they'd run out so much line that it would inevitably catch in the mouth of another fish, cutting it as if with a scissors—an expensive proposition when using costly lures. The breakoff problem could be relieved a tad by using 50-pound-test mono shock leaders and soft plastic lures, which are more affordable.

Outside the discharge boat anglers would be wise to check out White Rock and Two Tree Rocks, the first two rock structures that stick above the surface as a boat is brought around the corner at Millstone Point. Two Tree Channel is quite a ways offshore. The shallow shelves of 24 to 40 feet deep around Two Tree Rocks provide excellent fluke drifts, with the rocky high spots providing the type of habitat that attracts blackfish, bluefish, and striped bass as well.

A short distance offshore and to the east of Millstone Point, lined up almost perfectly with the shoreline of Pleasure Beach's stone jetties, is Bartlett Reef. This boomerang-shaped reef juts up off the bottom, with some surface rocks sticking up out of about 40 to 50 feet of water. Its presence causes a rip current over the top of the reef in 2 to 15 feet of water that creates one of the best striped bass/bluefish reefs in the area. Bartlett Reef holds striped bass throughout the season, with the spring and fall migrations being especially productive for bigger fish.

During the spring run in late May or early June, anglers catch huge bass on lures such as Yozuri Hydro Squirts, large Slug-Gos, McKala or Luhr Jensen soft plastic 3- or 4-inch squids, bucktails, swimming plugs, Salt Shakers, and poppers. Squid imitations are best at this time of year. In later summer live eels, live hickory shad, or trolling the reef with large swimming plugs or tube and worm rigs is the best way to consistently catch jumbo stripers.

JORDAN COVE

To the east of Millstone Point lies Jordan Cove, which, like Niantic Bay, is a narrow finger of water cut off from the Sound by a road. The bridge over the cove provides angler access for what is a small, limited fishery. In season some striped bass are caught off this bridge, especially after dark on an ebb tide. Jordan Cove itself, however, is most popular during spring and late fall as a winter flounder spot. It is one of the few small estuaries in the area that continues to produce at least a few winter flounder each season, mostly in spring. In summer the bridge is a destination for anglers after snapper blues and, after dark, blue crabs.

PLEASURE BEACH PARK AND DOCK ROAD STATE LAUNCH

Pleasure Beach, a small town beach for Waterford residents, shares a parking area with the Dock Road State Launch. Dock Road is most easily reached off exit 81, the Cross Road exit from I-95. Head south to Route 1, then east on Route 1; double back onto Route 156 west for a short distance, and make a left (south) turn onto Route 213 south (toward the Sound). Go right onto Goshen Road and onto Dock Road, following signs to the launch. It is a steep concrete ramp that can handle two boats at once and has parking for 45 trailers. Like all the other state launch sites, it becomes overloaded on weekends. Dock Road Launch provides the shortest boat run to Bartlett Reef and the productive rocky shorelines to the east. It is the second shortest run to the Race and the fastest, most direct shot to Little and Great Gull Islands and the Sluiceway.

The rocky breakwalls and riprap at this access point are often utilized successfully by shore-based anglers who catch stripers, bluefish, fluke, flounder, snapper blues, blackfish, and porgies on a regular basis. It is one of the few shore-based places anglers can go with a reasonable expectation of hooking into the false albacore that constantly run through this area from August through October.

HARKNESS MEMORIAL STATE PARK

To reach Harkness Memorial State Park, head straight on Route 213 past the turn to Dock Road Launch. Harkness Park provides walk-in angler access after dark, which—combined with its tide-swept rocky shoreline, complete with sand beach and inflowing salt pond—makes this one of the more productive shore-based public fishing spots in eastern Connecticut. A cadre of regulars fish the tides here for striped bass, bluefish, fluke, winter flounder, blackfish, and porgies with periods of good success punctuated by droughts when the fish are not in along the shore. Overall this is a very fishy spot. The tidal pond on the western edge of the park also holds some blue crabs for crabbers to play around with, and the cut where it flows into

Casting from the beach at Harkness State Park. Harkness is one of the state's best places to surf fish from public property.

the Sound is a fish magnet. Anglers often take fluke here by casting small jigs baited with squid strips or live mummies along the current lines when the tide is ebbing from the pond.

Because swimming is not allowed at the park, the entire shoreline, including the sand beach, is open to fishing year-round. There is a fee to park during the day, but after dark anglers can park and walk a pretty fair distance to the water and fish.

Harkness Park is only a couple of miles east of Pleasure Beach off Route 213, in the town of Waterford.

OCEAN BEACH PARK

Ocean Beach is a public swimming beach complete with mezzanine, rides, and mini golf—a decent place to take the family if a day for everyone is the objective. The problem is, the fishing is best before and after anyone would want to go swimming. Anglers can fish the beach only during the off season. At the western end of the boardwalk, however, lies Alewife Cove, which drains into the Sound along a rocky ledge and over a rock-strewn drop-off. The result is an excellent, little-known fishing spot that holds striped bass and fluke as long as these species are in the area. It also produces bluefish, snapper blues, winter flounder (rarely), and blackfish off the rocks, though most anglers fishing this spot are casting lures for blues and bass. If weakfish ever return to the region in numbers, this would be a good place to look for them.

This is an easy access point for fly rodders and anglers casting light spinning tackle. After dark a few "sharpies" sling eels into the outflow on the ebb tide with good success during summer and fall. This is a great place to toss a popper, shallow swimmer, swimming jig, or soft plastic such as a Slug-Go or Fin-S fish rigged without any additional weight.

6

The Thames River

One of eastern Connecticut's premier fishing destinations is the Thames River. More like a large cove or fjord than the hard-flowing, classic rivers such as the Connecticut or Housatonic, the Thames is created by the confluence of the Yantic and Shetucket Rivers to make a 45-foot-deep harbor in Norwich. From there a 20- to 25-foot-deep channel cuts its way toward the Sound through a wide, shallow river basin with numerous inflowing streams, each choked off from the river by railroad tracks, creating a shallow cove inside.

Many of the major tributary streams support alewife runs. This food source—combined with anadromous runs of American shad, hickory shad, gizzard shad, and annual influxes of menhaden—makes for a very "fishy" spot due to the constant presence of forage in the form of adult clupeids and (later in summer) their fingerlings as they head out to the ocean. In addition, the river abounds with silversides, mummichogs, grass shrimp, eels, crabs, and of course worms. A veritable smorgasbord, it attracts and holds all species of marine, anadromous, and freshwater fish throughout the course of a year.

Perhaps the most interesting aspect of the Thames River is the fact that it has one of the largest—if not *the* largest—non-

Eric Covino measures and displays a 25-pound-plus Thames River striper that hit during a snow squall one cold day in February.

spawning, overwintering populations of striped bass anywhere in the country. You can catch striped bass, often big striped bass, literally any day of the year from the waters of the Thames, providing you know where to cast your line.

The wintering population of stripers is really part of the fall migration. Tagging information indicates that the Thames River fish may return here each year to spend the winter (at least while they are juveniles or young adults), then move on to their natal river (probably the Hudson) to spawn. Some may drop their eggs in the Thames, but its physical characteristics are not conducive to striper survival, so odds are that none makes it past egg or early larval stages.

It appears that some of the fish may even intentionally return "home" to the Thames each winter, while others are simply part of the coastal migration that happened to swim up into the river to feed in fall, before becoming trapped when winter swept into the region. Once cold winter water temperatures take over the area, the fish in the Thames become stranded, so to speak. As winter takes over, they generally move upriver, where they concentrate and spend the months of December through March or early April in the upper third of the Thames, moving into and out of Norwich Harbor with the changing tides.

The bass move up into the harbor with the flood tide, where they stack up into incredibly dense schools. Depth finder images have shown these superdense schools to be anywhere from 15 to as much as 40 feet thick, in 45 feet of water. I saw that last one with my own eyes, or I would not have believed it. The screen looked like we were running aground—in the center of Norwich Harbor, where it's 45 to 46 feet deep at high tide! It was sunny, and water clarity wasn't bad. I peered over the side of the boat; just below, a dense "black cloud" of stripers could be seen for more than an hour, until the dropping tide "siphoned" them on downriver.

Generally, wintering schools of bass tend to average 10 to 20 feet thick when concentrated in Norwich Harbor. These schools certainly number in the thousands, perhaps tens of thousands of fish according to some rough, underwater video-aided estimations I have made in the past.

Most of the bass caught during the winter reflect the general size and age structure of the population in the region during fall, with most being schoolies ranging from 14 to 24 inches. However, fish up to 40 pounds have been caught from the Thames during the dead of winter. My personal best dead-of-winter striped bass from the river is about 10 pounds short of that mark.

Fishermen can catch these wintering stripers from the town docks in downtown Norwich, just off Route 2 as it passes by the gazebo on the harbor where the Shetucket River enters, under the Laurel Hill bridge. There is parking at the town park on the river, or across the street in the municipal lot for a small fee. Anglers fishing from the docks during winter catch most of their fish on chunk baits, sandworms, or jigs that are cast into the current where the Shetucket River enters the harbor. As is always the case with stripers, even during the chill of winter, they hit better under low-light conditions or after dark.

At the town access area you'll find a single-bay, concrete launch that is open year-round. It is occasionally unusable when blocked by ice during the coldest stretches of winter. During cold winters, boat-fishing anglers can be iced off the Thames for a month or more. Due to tidal influences, which erode sheet ice, the river can be fished from shore almost any day of the year. Call the Fish Connection at 860-885-1739 before venturing to the Thames River during the winter months for a report on accessibility and how the bass are biting.

Winter striper action is fastest early in the season—from late November, when they first begin concentrating in the lower to middle sections of the channel, through mid-February when dead-of-winter cold temperatures settle into the water column. After this point fishing activity slows overall, though it may be productive on one day when conditions are good, then quickly turn around and become lousy for the next four or five days. The worst fishing—just as in summer—is when the skies are clear and the winds blow cold and hard from the north, under the influence of winter high-pressure systems. "Bluebird" weather is always better for picnicking than fishing.

Wintering striped bass can be caught under most weather conditions, though like stripers it's usually more a matter of how many, rather than "did you get one" when fishing from a boat. Shore fishermen must wait for the tides to come up, pushing the bass within casting distance of the town docks.

The best fishing conditions during daylight hours are found on overcast days when the temps are mild and the barometer is low or dropping. Cold, windy, high-pressure days make for the most challenging fishing, despite the fact that you may literally bounce your lures off the heads of thousands of bass during the course of a day. The absolute hottest action in winter, especially for the shore-based anglers, is during or just after warm winter rains (if they don't cause floods or extremely fast river flows) or extended periods of midwinter thaw.

In March or early April water temperatures begin to rise, helped along by the sun's heating effect on the extensive shallow flats that border the lower two-thirds of the river channel. Once water temperatures break 50 degrees, things fire back up as dense wintering schools of bass break up and move downriver to feed. Some of these fish move out to the ocean to continue their migration to spawning areas in New York or possibly Chesapeake Bay, which had been curtailed in fall. Others simply begin prowling the shallow and warming flats and shorelines for food. The bigger stripers key in on the spawning runs of alewives that usually show up in the Thames sometime in late March, while smaller stripers take what they can find in the form of free-living isopods, worms, mummichogs, and other sources of nutrition.

For winter fishing, boat anglers should have a fish finder to locate the densely packed schools of bass. Despite their impressive size, when the tide is running these schools move surprisingly fast and can quickly disappear from underneath the boat. Wintering schools of stripers tend to concentrate and build up in the deepest part of Norwich Harbor with the flood tide before stringing out downriver, often as far as the Mohegan Sun Casino and Pequot bridge in Uncasville with the ebb. This pattern holds true for most of the winter, with breaks occurring around extreme weather conditions and storms.

Overwintering striped bass school much more tightly packed together than during the rest of the year. Schools in the harbor are often so densely packed that they appear as a solid black wall—often with a gray line that rookies may mistake for the bottom—on a depth finder. We call this phenomenon "the building" or "the wall" due to the often extreme, wall-like edges the schools create.

The odd thing is, these schools are not there to feed, as a school of bass that shows up on a depth finder screen during the summer would be doing. They are just waiting the winter out, doing minimal feeding, due to reduced metabolic rates and hence reduced nutritional demands.

Once you've located schools, you can catch fish by trolling small deep-diving plugs through the schools. We have done well using 4½-inch-long Bomber Deep A's with 10-pound-test Fireline. On a fast troll that makes the rod tip dance, the Deep A's will dive down 18 to 22 feet—enough to run right through the center of the bass in all but the deepest parts of the harbor.

Most anglers choose to catch wintering bass using light spinning or bait-casting tackle and various forms of jigs. The exact style isn't terribly important, though normally narrow-profile, brightly colored jigs that are 2½ to 4½ inches long are most effective. Many anglers do well using small white or chartreuse Mister Twister tails on jigheads that are heavy enough to reach the bottom. I have had the best success using a Road Runner jighead ranging from ½ to 1 ounce, hair trimmed off, with a 4½-inch Fin-S fish or Salt Shaker (shad-type body) soft plastic teaser in natural shiner, white, or chartreuse colors.

The key here, as in any sort of jig fishing, is to match the weight of the jig to drift and current speed. Always use the lightest possible jig that will reach and hold the bottom when casting or drift fishing for any species of fish.

Over the past few years a few hard-core winter bass fishermen have adapted deep, open-water summertime fishing tactics—such as wire-line trolling techniques—to the river with great success. They troll slowly, using small spreader rigs with multiple hooks with 3- to 4-inch tubes or Shad Bodies with 20-pound-test Monel wire or lead-core lines set back roughly 125 feet. Wire trolls deeper, and gets there faster, than lead core. Wire-line trolling will usually take fish when all other methods fail. Though effective, catching small school stripers on a pool-cue rod and wire line isn't the most thrilling method of taking stripers. In the right hands, however, it accounts for some of the best catches each winter in both number of fish per hour and top-end size. When winter fishing is on in the Thames River, anglers who know what they are doing can land incredible numbers of stripers with very little effort. Our record catch (and release) was 176 school bass of up to about 28 inches in four and a half hours of fishing with three anglers, using light spinning tackle and jigs.

Captain Al Anderson of the charter boat *Prowler* out of Snug Harbor, Rhode Island, is the expert when it comes to catching stripers using these techniques in summer off Block Island or Montauk Point and during winter in the Thames River. They have accounted for thousands of the Littoral Society tags he has placed in stripers over the past decades.

While it's the most unusual fishery the Thames River provides, winter bass is far from the only one. In addition to striped bass, bluefish chase bait upriver to Norwich Harbor beginning in late June or July most years, and often hang around until Thanksgiving. Of course snapper blues invade late every summer.

Weakfish often move into the mouth of the river during late summer along with fluke—which have been caught on chunk baits intended for bluefish off Buoy 27 at least 7 miles upriver from the Sound. Fluke fishing is especially good in the lower Thames River when peanut bunker are plentiful and moving miles upriver. Fluke follow, concentrating and feeding, often unscathed by anglers who pass overhead on their way out of the river to fish the Sound for this very species.

One year when testing out my personal theories on late-summer/early-fall, shallow-water fluke-fishing methods, a friend and I landed and released nearly 70 fluke to about 4 pounds in half an ebb tide in the Montville stretch of the Thames. Our method was to find baby bunker schools, then either drift through or anchor in their midst and work the fluke using quarter-ounce Luhr Jensen fluorescent B-2 Squid jigs baited with a short strip of squid and (until they ran out) an Arkansas shiner (the minnow bait anglers use for freshwater fishing) or live mummichog.

In fall, when peanut bunker draw all species of predators into the river, anglers fishing from both shore and boat will experience some of the most incredible fishing action on blitzing bass and bluefish anywhere. Depending on the tides and location of bait, the blitzes can take place anywhere in the river. Provided that the weather remains stable, without any major temperature changes or flooding rains, this window of excellent fishing can last for a month or more, beginning in the river mouth and sometimes working its way upriver as far as Norwich Harbor with the flood tide.

The upper third of the Thames River channel is bordered by propeller-eating rock walls that require some vigilance to avoid, with or without a chart. When the tide is high, bass and blues often push bait over these walls and corner them inside these corral-like structures in 2 to 4 feet of water. The carnage this phenomenon creates makes for some exciting light-tackle, shallow-water fishing action that rivals any popular surf spot along the coast. For all tackle needs and up to date info on the Thames visit the Fish Connection on Route 12, 2 miles south of Norwich.

The lower Thames, where the water is salty and deep, provides excellent fishing for blackfish and porgies in season. The bridge abutments, rock piles, docks, and ledges outside the river's mouth all provide excellent blackfish habitat during both the spring and fall runs. Normally blackfish action inside the protection of New London Harbor takes place from October through Thanksgiving. The harbor provides anglers with a place to hide when the nearly constant winds brought by Mother Nature as fall slips into winter are howling too hard for effective or safe fishing out in the Sound.

Upriver, below the Greenville Dam north of Norwich on the Shetucket River, anglers catch American shad, herring, hickory shad, carp, both species of black bass, white perch, yellow perch, pumpkinseeds, bluegills, redbreast sunfish, pickerel, and even the occasional northern pike or adult Atlantic salmon that drops down from the stocking program upriver. This is in addition to a fabulous spring striper fishery.

Each spring these freshwater species are joined by striped bass that are drawn to the base of the Greenville Dam by migrating herring and minnows such as spot-tail shiners. These bass include overwintering fish that stick around for the food and migrants from outside the river on their annual spring run to the north. This fishery is for large to average-sized fish, up to nearly 40 pounds, along with run-of-the-mill schoolies. Back before the stripers were fished to oblivion, 40- to 50-pound-

This is me holding a 15-or-so-pound striper that hit a herring clone (10-inch Fin-S fish) during the spring herring run at Greenville Dam on the Thames River, Norwich.

ers were not uncommon every spring in the upper Thames and Shetucket to the base of Greenville Dam.

From the time the wintering schools break up each spring and spread out to prowl the river's food-rich shallows, continuing through the summer, anglers take stripers along the entire course of the Thames. In spring and fall big fish are often mixed in. As in all major coastal rivers in the region, after summer temperature regimes take over, the larger fish move out to sea, leaving smaller, more temperature-tolerant schoolies and (later on) bluefish to do battle with anglers upriver as far as Norwich Harbor.

Shore fishing for all these species can be found in Norwich Harbor, along most of the shore between Poquetanuck Cove Trestle (locally known as the drawbridge) to the pullover at Buoy 27 at the south end of the mile-long straightaway on Route 12, Gales Ferry. You can also find fishing off Dock Road; at a turn toward the river off Power House Road off Route 32 in Montville; Stoddard Wharf State Launch off Route 12 (cartoppers and canoes only) in Preston/Ledyard; on either side of the I-95 overpass in Groton/New London; as well as at various spots in New London. The best shore fishing access is at the new public fishing pier south of the train station in New London and at the Fort Trumbull State Access, where there is a second, excellent fishing pier farther downriver in New London Harbor near Shaws Cove. Various other shore-based spots are private and can't be mentioned here, but they can be fished by small numbers of anglers without any problems.

As water flows slow in spring and temps rise, bigger bass leave coastal rivers and estuaries first, often leaving small schoolies like this one behind to have fun with. This fish was caught on a fly below the Greenville Dam, Norwich, but the scene could be below any dam on any coastal river in the region during May or early June.

Boat launches are located in downtown Norwich off Route 2 in the harbor; off Dock Road, Montville; and under the I-95 bridge on both sides of the river in Groton and New London. To reach the Thames River Launch in New London, take exit 84 off I-95 and go left onto Williams Street, then east onto State Pier Road; continue to the end under the bridge. To reach the Kenneth Streeter State Boat Launch in Groton, take exit 85 off I-95, then turn right onto Bridge Street and right again onto Fairview Avenue, which runs north along the river. The launch is a left under the bridge near the railroad tracks.

Anglers launching or running out of the various marinas in the area will find excellent fishing along the shore from Ocean Beach to Pleasure Beach west of the river. Offshore from these areas are Sarah Ledge, Goshen Reef, and Waterford Reef, plus loads of rocky structure. Out in front of the Thames River's mouth lies the New London Lighthouse. To the east you'll find excellent structure around Frank Ledge, Black Ledge, and the rocky shoreline that lines Eastern Point.

OTHER ACCESS POINTS IN GROTON
Bluff Point State Reserve

Of interest not only to fishermen but to hikers and nature lovers as well is Bluff Point State Reserve, located on Depot Road, a southern turn toward the ocean off Route 1 in Groton. Bluff Point is an 800-plus-acre piece of coastal, upland habitat, the only spot like it in the state that has not been developed. There is a shallow brackish cove—the Poquonnock River—which is filled from the Groton Reservoirs. The brook leading to the reservoirs supports an active herring run that in spring draws some jumbo stripers into this long, shallow arm of the sea for a couple of weeks.

Striped bass can be caught in the Poquonnock River itself for most of summer and fall, though during the hottest months most of the action will take place near its mouth at Pine Island

and Bush Point, where this unique estuary meets the sea, or out around the rocky tip of Bluff Point itself.

The shoreline along the coast of Bluff Point has a long rock/sand beach and a rugged, rocky, fish-filled shoreline that leads into shallow sandy Mumford Cove to the east. Offshore from Bluff Point is a triangle of shoals that includes Seaflower Reef, Vixen Ledge, and Horseshoe Reef—a dangerous, shallow rock pile that has eaten the props of many an unsuspecting powerboater and angler who thought that because he was half a mile offshore, he was out of harm's way. Fluke fishing is excellent from May on around all of these "high" spots. Most years Vixen Ledge or Seaflower Reef produces some of the largest doormat fluke weighed in at area bait-and-tackle shops.

Seaflower Reef is straight offshore from Horseshoe Reef, which can be seen abovewater during low tide. This hump comes up out of 30 to 40 feet of water to within less than 12 feet of the surface, with shallow arms extending north and east from the high point of the reef. The result is a fluke-attracting-and-holding structure that always produces some excellent catches of summer flounder. Beyond Seaflower Reef and stretching across the Sound to North Hill, Fishers Island, New York, is a series of deep holes and humps that have the potential to yield some monster fluke.

While I was filling in on a research trawler employed by the Connecticut DEP, Marine Fisheries Unit, a trawl pulled through one of the deep holes near North Dumpling Island produced the largest fluke I have ever seen—a monster that was 34 to 35 inches and perhaps 14 or 15 pounds! It was released alive and healthy after being recorded on our data sheets.

Bluff Point State Park is one of the nicer surf-fishing places in the state, but getting to the water requires a 1-mile walk from the free public parking area at the entrance to the reserve. No camping is allowed, though many fishermen make the walk and spend the night fishing the surf for stripers and blues. The rocks also harbor some large blackfish and porgies, while the adjacent sand beaches can be worked for fluke in summer, and for winter flounder in spring.

A long curved cove created by the swing of the tides runs from Pine Island, along Brushy Point and Bluff Point Beaches, to Bluff Point. Like Pleasure Beach to the west of the Thames, it's an area that attracts and often holds small tuna in late summer. They are not usually within range of surf casters working the beaches and rocky shores, but certainly are vulnerable to anglers who fish the area from boats.

Up inside the Poquonnock River off South Road (a southerly turn off Route 1 in Groton) lies the Groton Town Park Recreation Area, which has a small launch site where anglers can drop small boats to fish the cove or poke out into the Sound around Pine Island, Avery Point, or the Bluff Point and its long rocky beach.

The Poquonnock River is one of the last remaining (somewhat) productive winter flounder spots. During late winter and early spring, when flatfish are spawning just after ice-out, the upper portion of the river becomes the area's hottest winter flounder destination for about two or three weeks. Historically it was always a good spot, and one of the few shore-based fishing areas that continues to produce winter flounder for those who try during late March and early April.

The Poquonnock River in Groton is also a great spot to catch blue crabs in summer, and one of the few clean, easily accessible clam beds in the state that is open for most of the season. To the east, Mumford Cove and the Lagoon at Groton Long Point provide good crabbing to people entering from the sea in small craft. Unfortunately shore access to the lagoon, its bridges, and its breakwall is limited to residents only.

Bayberry Land State Launch

One of the major state launch sites in eastern Connecticut is found in Groton off Bayberry Lane, a short distance west of Bluff Point. It is reached by taking exit 87 off I-95, then following

Shennecossett Road along the Thames and the coast. Take the sharp bend to the east as it hooks past Eastern Point and the University of Connecticut campus at Avery Point, then take a right (south) turn onto Bayberry Lane. The launch site parking area can be seen from the road before the turn. This is a quality launch that holds 65 cars. Unfortunately it's also a very busy one that becomes overfilled on weekends and holidays. Bayberry Lane offers perhaps the shortest boat run on the Connecticut coast to the great fishing of the Race Point end of Fishers Island and "inside" Fishers Island itself. There are some low-water concerns at dead low tide when the moon is full.

7

The Mystic River and Groton Long Point

The smallest watershed of the seven major coastal rivers that cut into the Connecticut coastline is the Mystic River. A major historic and shopping destination, the town of Mystic draws hundreds of thousands of visitors each year to its Mystic Seaport Whaling Museum, Mystic Aquarium, and numerous popular shops ranging from small stalls downtown to factory outlets near the aquarium. Though an area of excellent fishing, it is often overlooked—even by local anglers, who tend to drive through on their way to major offshore fishing areas such as the Race to the south or the Watch Hill Reef Complex to the east. The waters in and adjacent to the Mystic River provide top-notch fishing for striped bass, bluefish, fluke, blackfish, and porgies, with some limited fishing for weakfish, small tuna, and winter flounder.

During the cold months from November through late March, sea-run brown trout can be caught in the upper portion of this estuary where Whitford Brook enters in Old Mystic.

Whitford Brook was one of the original sea-run brown trout streams stocked by the state DEP back in the late 1960s and early 1970s. There was a period during the late 1970s when the area north of I-95 was productive for sea-run browns, from ice-out until temps warmed up in spring. Unfortunately, as in all of the state's sea-run streams, fishing waned—though it never disappeared completely—after the sea-run program was terminated in the late 1970s. There were always some drop-downs and remnant, barely catchable populations of brown trout in the upper Mystic River due to stocking of fingerling browns in Whitford Brook.

As of 2002, stocking of trout in the upper river has resumed in an effort to re-create a fishable population of sea-runs in Whitford Brook as well as the Saugatuck River, Oil Mill Brook, and Latimer Brook, in the upper Niantic River, East Lyme; Mianus River, Greenwich; Hammonassett River, Madison; Farm River, Branford; and Eight Mile River, East Haddam/Lyme.

Mystic, looking over Mason Island and into Fishers Island Sound. Mystic is one of the most protected estuaries in the state. Tides flow at all angles, making it a great area for fluke. Its food-rich shoals attract striped bass, with a worm hatch in spring, holding bass all season long, plus bluefish, weakfish, hickory shad, fluke, and winter flounder. Porgies are outside on the rocks and snapper blues are plentiful off any dock or bridge in late summer.

Fishing for sea-runs is seasonal, starting in November when they come into these rivers to spawn. From then until warm water drives them to the Sound sometime late in March, they can be caught anytime the waters are ice-free. Generally the best fishing takes place beginning around ice-out in spring. They are most readily caught on live mummichogs, with flies and other classic trout lures.

These are elusive fish that respond best to very light-tackle and thin, light lines. In the past I had my best hookup rates on 2-pound-test line, but sometimes lost fish due to snap-offs on rocks or in eelgrass. With the advent of superstrong lines such as Fireline in 4-pound test, breakoffs should no longer pose a problem, so go as light as the superlines and your tackle allow.

Historically the Mystic River was once a prime winter flounder fishing area from late fall through early summer. I can remember catching flounder in good numbers during late March and April from the docks (which are now closed to angling) in downtown Mystic, then later in summer catching all we wanted for a few meals in the lower river from Clam Point out past Noank Ship Yard, toward Groton Long Point and Horseshoe Reef. During that same time period Palmer Cove, Groton Long Point Lagoon, and Mumford Cove were all loaded with winter flounder as well. Anglers once caught good numbers of flatfish off the bridge over Palmer Cove, but those days are gone.

Despite limited and decent winter flounder fishing off nearby Bluff Point, the winter flounder population in the Mystic River has not recovered very well. There have only been very limited and unimpressive reports of winter flounder action from this area for more than a decade.

Shore-based angler access in this entire area—the yuppie capital of eastern Connecticut—ranges from limited to nonexistent. In fact, only a few bridges, trestles, and small stretches of coastal land that cannot be specified here are fished tentatively by general angling public. The town dock in Noank is a classic example. People could be dropped off to fish, but parking is difficult at this town access point. Six Penny Island, up inside the river in West Mystic, is another example of a good public access point that is difficult to reach. Parking here is near the sewage pump station on the tide flats to the northern end of Bee Bee Cove, off Route 215 heading into Mystic.

Anglers visiting the area can rent boats at Shaffer's Marina, Mystic south onto Ocean Drive (the road to Mason Island) off Route 1, at the second light east of town on top of a small ridge. Boat rentals are also available at Wild Bill's Marina off Noank River Road, a left turn just past the spot where Route 215 heads north toward Mystic from Groton. The Sound presents a spectacular view as you drive down what is known as the Groton Long Point or Long Hill Road. Both of these marinas also provide the only small, private launch sites in this area, with a nominal launch fee for people who do not dock boats at the premises.

This lack of easy access is the primary reason many anglers ignore the great fishing to be found in and around the mouth of

My son Jared caught this small school bass on his first cast off the spire at Groton Long Point. Schoolies are easy to catch and a great species on which to teach a young angler how to handle lures or flies.

this river. The glaciers did a great job of scouring out rocky islands and leaving rock piles, points, and coves throughout this complex little estuary.

Striped bass can be caught off the mouth, as well as upriver into Mystic proper, from late April through early November, with perhaps a small number of fish overwintering here, as they do in nearly every other deep, protected estuary along the coast.

Small boats, kayaks, and canoes can fish the river channel, with the best fishing being where coves such as Bee Bee Cove dump into the river with changing tides. Also, the flats along the river channel provide rich food sources for hungry stripers, including a worm spawn that takes place late in May every year, usually three or four days on either side of May 22.

Off the mouth of the river Ram Island, Mouse Island, Whaleback Rock, White Rock, Gates Island, Ellis Reef, Cormorant Rocks, and the Monastery, along with the channels in between, all provide great habitat that holds striped bass and fluke throughout the season.

Ram Island Reef is one of those minor big-bass areas that can be red hot or dead cold. It's one of those places that needs to be put on your "paper route" and checked out on every trip to the area. In the past we've had a night when three of us caught more than 20 stripers of 15 to nearly 40 pounds on live eels between midnight and dawn on the dropping tide, then returned a week later to get skunked. It's all in the timing, because this is not one of those major reefs that always gives up big fish, though they may be present for a good portion of the season.

With some of the best striper-fishing hot spots anywhere within a 7- to 10-mile run of Mystic, most anglers bypass this lesser area for the glory spots. When it comes to taking fluke during the summer season, however, Mystic is one of the areas in which to drift—though it's difficult due to the tremendous amount of boat traffic moving around the lower river, particularly on a nice summer day. The most practical time to drift the narrow channels around the lower river and Ram Island is when boat traffic drops off due to rains or high winds in the Sound.

The mouth of the river is unique in its shape due to its split channel. The main channel runs straight out into the Sound between Mouse Island—a small rock with a single house perched precariously on its summit less than 10 feet above the tides—and Whaleback Rock, then out past Groton Long Point, in a generally north–south direction. The second channel separates from the main channel near Noank Shipyard and swings northeast, then east, creating a long run where the waters flow east–west.

Given that successful fluke fishing is totally dependent on having a good drift with wind and tides aligned, rather than against each other, the unique shape of this split channel means that most of the time it's possible to set up drifts with prevailing wind and tides. For this reason the lower Mystic River can usually be fished effectively under nearly any combination of wind and tide. The trick is watching the Weather Channel and planning ahead as to which tide will be the best to fish.

There are times when the majority of the fluke east of Niantic seem to settle into the Mystic/Groton area, especially early in the season when they first enter the Sound from the east entrance past Watch Hill.

You can fish both channels and well up inside the river as far as the railroad bridge. At the mouth, extensive flats adjacent to the channel create miles of the drop-off habitat into various channels that fluke like so much. The green marker buoy off Groton Long Point, where the channel enters the deeper water of Long Island Sound, marks an excellent triangular-shaped area—roughly half a mile long on each leg and away from the worst of the boat traffic—in which to catch fluke all summer long. There is also a great deep-water drift outside and approaching the shoals that create Ram Island Reef.

Ram Island Reef is the prime "outside spot" in the Mystic area. Swept with strong tides, it is a fish-attracting place with waters ranging from the top of the reef—which cuts the surface at low tide—to a 10- to 25-foot-deep hump that connects it to Ram Island itself. Inside the hump is a shoal area with a couple of deeper spots where big bass come to feed after dark. To the east is flat bottom ranging from 20 to 40 feet deep.

Ram Island Reef is a favorite porgy-fishing spot for the rental fleet that runs out of Shaffer's Marina and Wild Bill's. Anglers also drift for fluke in the deeper, sandy stretches around the high places. After dark, striper fishermen set up on anchor with rigged squid or chunk baits on wire or lead-core line. Some troll plugs or jigs off the reef, while others choose to drift live eels or live hickory shad over the reef in an effort to hook into those jumbo bass that are usually around from late May through fall.

The Mystic River, from Clam Point to Groton Long Point, holds one of the better clam beds in the area, though access is from boats only. Recently it has been raped by commercial tongers and clam dredges. Inside the Mystic River, its shoals and small coves all make excellent blue crabbing habitat in summer. Again, there is limited access from shore, but launching a small boat from one of the marinas can get a crabber into some excellent shallow, clear-water habitat that is perfect for fire lighting after dark (a practice that is legal in Connecticut but illegal in Rhode Island).

8

The Stonington Area

The port of Stonington is home to a large portion of Connecticut's small, but vocal, commercial fishing fleet. As in a good portion of Connecticut coastal towns, angler access is poor due to the fact most of the waterfront has been in private ownership since colonial times. In the town of Stonington itself, however, there are three places where nonresidents can cast a line from shore.

The first is a seasonal spot with poor parking, the Route 1A bridge over Quiambaug Cove. Before winter flounder fell off the region's fishing menu, this was one of those small, late-winter/early-spring spots that produced a few postspawn winter flounder—but not anymore. Like so many of the small estuaries that once produced winter flounder, it has pretty much dried up since the 1980s, when the last of the once extensive local winter flounder population was vacuumed off the bottom of Block Island Sound by the region's commercial trawling fleet.

This access point to Quiambaug Cove is still used by snapper bluefish anglers and blue crabbers in late summer, however. It is also a place that could produce some schoolie bass action during peak periods in spring and fall. I have personally seen 20- to 30-inch stripers all the way up inside this small, shallow cove feeding on a huge crop of needlefish one night while crabbing during the late 1990s.

There is a small pullover access along the extreme northern end of Quiambaug Cove right on Route 1, just before the turn toward Stonington at Main Street. Three to five cars can be seen parked on the shoulder, with their drivers crowded onto a small, broken-down dike over a tide marsh; here fishermen take some snapper blues on the top of the tide, and crabs throughout the season. With effort a small cartop boat or canoe can be dropped into the cove for crabbing without drawing the wrath of any landowners. Actually, Connecticut riparian law allows for people of the state to walk and fish anywhere along the coast below the mean high-tide mark, because by law Connecticut's intertidal shore belongs to the people of the state, not individuals. This zone is considered "Public Trust," and people fishing in it are not trespassing providing they don't step on dry land above the high-tide mark.

Farther down Quiambaug Cove, the railroad trestle provides better striper fishing, but this is difficult to access, is much more dangerous, and should not be utilized given the very silent high-speed trains that rip through the area.

The Stonington town dock is the location of the fish house where the commercial trawlers bring their catch to be packed and shipped on a daily basis. You can park and fish off the end of this dock but must keep away from the boat slips and boats themselves.

The blood, slurry, fish parts, and discarded or dropped fish that often find their way into the water from the docks attract some big stripers every summer. Though fishing in their primary feeding area is prohibited, they cruise around enough to make it an interesting place for anglers who know these fish are present and have the proper tackle and baits to catch them. Many a story from excited but empty-handed fishermen has come from this dock. Typically a big fish grabs a bait or lure, only to run a slalom course through the barnacle-encrusted pilings that support the piers and loading docks.

For the hungry, nearby is Skipper's Dock—a popular and locally famous eatery and bar that is accessible both by boat and by land.

The town pier in Stonington is a fair-to-middling striper and bluefish destination. It also produces some porgies, along with a smattering of fluke in summer. During the cold months, a rare winter flounder or two is caught from this once popular flatfish haven. Like all the other shore-based fishing in the region, it's most productive from sunset through dawn.

The best shore-based public access in the town of Stonington is Stonington Point, a turnaround at the end of Main Street that provides tourists and locals a spectacular view of Fishers Island Sound and Sandy Point Island. It is a scenic place from which to cast a line. Its rock-lined perimeter attracts stripers and blues, which are moving into and out of Stonington Harbor and nearby Little Narragansett Bay. When present, bluefish also move into this point to feed along the rip lines that set up when the tides change. As with any point of land, jetty, or pier in the region, during late summer it will produce some snapper blues.

Bottom fishermen will take blackfish from between the rocks during the spring season, porgies in summer, and winter flounder when water temps are dropping in fall or increasing in spring. During the heat of summer fluke will move past this location in the sandy bottom channels on either side. Hickory shad may be present to do battle later in summer, after water temperatures reach comfortable levels for this species.

Stonington Point is not known as a crabbing destination given its location on the deeper, cooler waters of the Sound, but I would keep a net handy during late summer: Prime crabbing grounds are located on either side of the point, so there is always the possibility of one passing by within scooping distance.

INSHORE BOAT AND SURF FISHING FROM STONINGTON TO WATCH HILL

To the east of Stonington borough but still in the township lies Barn Island State Park. Take exit 91 off I-95, head south, and take a left onto Main Street. Take a left (east) onto Route 1 and continue straight to the second light near the tail end of Wequetequock Cove, where the brook comes in and a stone house with a large round porthole window overlooks the cove and road. Take a right onto Greenhaven Road across the bridge, then a quick right onto Palmer Neck Road: The launch area is at the end of Palmer Neck Road. There is room for 65 trailers, with 10 or 15 more often parking in wide pullovers along the entrance road. This place fills quickly on weekends, so get there early or fish off hours to be assured of convenient parking. This is a narrow, almost single-lane, poorly maintained road, so watch your speed, take the hairpin turn over the railroad tracks slowly, and be courteous and considerate of oncoming traffic.

Barn Island, though on the coast, isn't really much of a fishing destination in itself; it's too shallow and muddy. Just past the bridge over the train tracks is a pullover and a couple-hundred-yard walk to the trestle over Wequetequock Cove. This bridge produces some school bass, snapper blues, and blue crabs in season. During the cold-weather months it also holds some tomcod and a long-shot chance for a winter flounder. Historically, when winters were cooler this was also a place to catch smelt—a fish that, even if it's present in places such as the Mystic River, the Thames River, Palmer Cove, and the Pawcatuck River, anglers have forgotten when and how to catch.

Barn Island access provides limited snapper bluefish opportunities off the small boat dock, which is not meant for fishing. The real potential for this important launch site—other than its obvious proximity to the Sound and nearby reefs—is access for small boats to take advantage of the excellent crabbing in the cove and tide marshes. During late fall and winter (when the season is open—something that doesn't take place every year) scalloping is allowed by permit from the Stonington Shellfish Commission in the shallows that dominate this tidal-marsh habitat. This depends, however, on whether there are enough scallops present to allow harvest. During years when scallop densities are too low, the season is not opened.

Anglers in small boats or kayaks can fish within the protected waters of Little Narragansett Bay, a shallow estuary protected from the open ocean by a long, barely-above-sea-level sand spit called Sandy Point. The Pawcatuck River, which is the primary freshwater source for this tidal estuary, splits into two channels that pass around either end of Sandy Point. The main deep channel heads west for about a mile between Sandy Point and the mainland, cutting a safe channel for larger boats before gouging a 39-foot-deep hole at the island's western tip. This hole holds fluke during summer months. It also attracts bait on the dropping tide, which in turn draws striped bass, bluefish, small tuna, and occasionally weakfish into the area to feed.

The secondary, unofficially marked shallow channel runs nearly straight out of the Pawcatuck River's mouth and parallel to the inside of Napatree Point. Marked by floats or pot buoys, this shallow channel lies between the eastern end of Sandy Point and Napatree Point, Rhode Island. Unless you're very familiar with the many shoals here, follow the channel markers in this shallow area between the island and shore as well as up inside the many shallow coves and bays within Little Narragansett Bay. Keep an eye peeled for breaks and working terns when running this channel, because during the season schools of bass and blues often feed in this area and can provide a quick jump-start or fun ending to any fishing trip.

The Rhode Island state line runs up the middle of Little Narragansett Bay, nearly splitting the main channel with Connecticut, to just short of the western end of Sandy Point Island before heading north, cutting off the extreme western tip of Sandy Point Island. Most of the island is in Rhode Island waters, but the deep hole at the tip and the fluke drifts up inside toward Barn Island are in Connecticut. This may seem trivial, but it can be important to anglers considering the many differences in the regulations governing popular species such as fluke, striped bass, and porgies between the two states.

The entire area around Sandy Point often offers excellent fishing for all the major species, including striped bass, bluefish, occasional weakfish, fluke, winter flounder, occasional black seabass, and, late in summer and fall, false albacore and bonito. Blackfish and porgies are less prevalent in this area because it is so shallow and sandy, lacking the rocks and deepwater cover these two species prefer.

Spawning runs of both American shad and herring head up into the Pawcatuck River, drawing early-run striped bass, some of considerable size, up as far as the dam in Westerly. Historically there have even been rare catches of sea-run brown trout, steelhead rainbow trout (which Rhode Island played around with in the upper Pawcatuck River), and possibly drop-down Atlantic salmon from stockings upstream. Later in spring and summer hickory shad and menhaden move into the river to provide predator drawing power for the remainder of the summer and fall angling season.

During the summer months, fluke slide into the shallows of the bay and around both sides of Sandy Point Island. The west channel and deep hole off Sandy Point are excellent areas in which to drift for fluke; the problem is the tremendous amount of boat traffic pouring out of the numerous marinas and yacht clubs inside the Pawcatuck River. For this reason, fishing in the channels and deep hole becomes something to do when fog or weather is keeping the majority of boaters in port. It is also a very good area to fish during the fall, when boat activity levels drop off after Labor Day.

In late summer and fall when peanut bunker, anchovies, silversides, or baby butterfish move into the shoals inside

Sandy Point, large schools of striped bass and bluefish typically follow them under the cover of darkness. In such conditions
small-boat anglers and kayakers often beach their boats on the
island and fish from shore after dark. On the seaward side, a
shallow sandbar can be waded for a long distance on the low
tide. Often bass and blues will push bait up against the island,
especially on a southern blow, making for some fast and fun
shallow-water fishing. Most often the best fishing will be found
from the stone abutment inside the island around the corner
from the deep hole and out around the western tip of the island,
where the channel runs out into the Sound. The best time for
this normally occurs between September and November,
depending on bait availability, weather, and water conditions.

Boats running out of Barn Island will have no problem
finding great fishing within a short run of Stonington. The two
breakwalls that guard Stonington Harbor both provide fish-
holding structure that attracts and holds blackfish, porgies,
and striped bass. The sand-bottomed areas around these rock
structures and the natural rock piles that make for dangerous
running off the north end of the eastern or "outer" breakwall
are excellent fluke-fishing areas, but are hampered by large
numbers of lobster pot buoys and tackle-eating ghost pots that
lie right in among the rocks.

The breakwalls are great places to cast for bass, blues,
and (later in summer) the small inshore tuna (false albacore
and bonito) that typically show up in late August or early
September.

Fluke fishermen may want to fish within the relatively protected waters of the Sound when conditions are kicking up outside. West of Stonington lies a visible landmark called White
Rock—a large rock that juts abovewater in front of Lords Point.
From there to the inner breakwall, there are some channels and
open drifts that are excellent for fluke.

Just outside Stonington Harbor and the breakwalls is a
deep hole that often holds small tuna (when they aren't raging

around the area), bass, porgies, fluke, and bluefish. Noyes Shoal—a shallow hump rising out of this hole—is a great fluke drift. Fish the edges of this high spot by trying different drifts until you locate fish, then maintain that drift and depth until the action subsides.

Heading east out of main channel (unless it's high water), be sure to run out and around the breakwall, because the flats inside the wall contain some major rocks near the north end and can be too shallow for safe running when tides are dead low.

The area east of the breakwall is called the Stonington Flats and features a uniformly sloping sand bottom that runs from the outer breakwall, where the hooter is fixed, eastward to Napatree Point, Rhode Island's southernmost tip of land. The flats average 10 to 15 feet deep and slope off into 30 to 45 feet of water. Because this area is swept with such strong tides—due to its location near the passages that drain Long Island Sound into the Atlantic—it is a superb fishing area for just about everything.

These extensive shallow, sandy areas, with varying depths, create some prime fluke-fishing habitat. Anglers who are most successful concentrate their drifts along the drop-offs and around the edges of holes and humps in this area. Napatree Point and the shoals offshore from it have been among the area's most popular and productive nearshore fluke-fishing grounds for generations. Anglers do best by drifting with the ebb tide and light west wind, parallel to the edges of the drop-offs, starting shallow and then running progressively deeper until fish are encountered. Typically the fluking rule holds true here as elsewhere: Big baits catch big fish, and bigger fish tend to hold in deeper water. One of the largest fluke I've seen caught on a rod and reel came from the shoals sloping down from Latimer Light. This true doormat weighed 12½ pounds and was 32 inches long, 14½ inches wide, and 3 inches thick! I'd love to take a fish like that, have a fiberglass mount made, put legs on it, and use it as a tacky end table.

When fishing is peaking, fluke will be caught all the way from the north end of the Stonington Breakwall into the channel running along the north side of Sandy Point, and out to the depths of the Sound between the Stonington Flats and Latimer Light. It's a flukey area.

9

Napatree Point
to Watch Hill

Napatree Point can be reached by following Route 1A out of Westerly, Rhode Island, parking in the municipal lot in Watch Hill, and walking out the long sandy beach that begins in town.

Napatree Point is itself a rock pile left by the glaciers that was filled in from land to its end by the shifting sands of the Pawcatuck River along its western edge. The result was a mile-long sand spit jutting from Watch Hill out into the waters of the Sound. During World War I a fort and gun emplacement was built at the end of Napatree Point to help guard the Sound against enemy invasion. When the powers-that-be realized that a boat could run in close to Watch Hill and get behind the fort, it was abandoned.

The fort now is a broken-down wreck that attracts adventurous beachgoers from popular Watch Hill Beach, a crescent-shaped strand that fish cruise constantly; it connects Napatree Point and Watch Hill Point. The tip of Napatree Point is a popular fishing spot for both boat and surf fishermen. Surf casters can park in Watch Hill and walk the mile to the tip of Napatree Point, where they can catch striped bass, bluefish, and possibly a weakfish during a good year, plus taking shots at the passing false albacore or bonito during late summer and fall. Bottom-fishermen will catch blackfish, porgies, seabass, and fluke. Again, winter flounder are pretty much off the fishing menu at present, but a spring trip could snag one.

Schools of bass and blues often push bait between Napatree Point and Watch Hill. During the off season, surf casters can walk the beaches following the fish, which tend to move with the tides. Most choose to sit and cast the rocky waters of both points. Both places are easily accessed by shore fishermen from designated parking areas in the town of Watch Hill. Do not park outside designated parking spots, because you will be ticketed, towed, or both, due to the high volume of traffic this small town absorbs during the tourist season. Nonanglers just don't understand.

For this reason many hard-core surf casters fish in spring before the beaches open or in fall after they close, to avoid the heavy traffic and parking hassles. In summer those who fish wait until after dark, when the traffic also dries up to a some degree.

Napatree Point is a prime nighttime, live-eel-fishing destination that produces some big bass from the surf every year. From a boat you can also cast live hickory shad or menhaden, if you can catch them up inside the Pawcatuck River. Chunk mackerel or fresh-cut pieces of hickory shad—which are easy to catch for bait in any of the area's salt ponds, estuaries, and embayments—have become a popular bait since the regional explosion in the population of this sporty member of the shad family.

Napatree Point is a great place to fish from a boat due to the variety of water depths and bottom types crammed into its relatively small area. When running around the point in a small boat, be aware that a couple of hundred yards to the east of Napatree Point, not quite in line with Watch Hill Light, lies a cluster of unmarked rocks that come up to within lower-unit-crunching depth of the surface. The charts say 3 feet, but I've seen it awash and showing like a sliver on moon tides, and know one unfortunate angler who lost a prop to these rocks. If you know where they are, it's a great place to throw a lure or live eel.

Lure casters do well on the classic lures including swimming plugs; Yozuri Swimmers, Mambo Minnows, and Wind Cheater Rebels are among the favorites. Poppers such as Creek Chub Chuggers (in chrome) and Atom Poppers are perhaps among the more popular surface lures, along with an odd lure called a Robert's Ranger, a teardrop-shaped slab that casts like a bullet and skips along the surface and just below on the retrieve. In recent years soft plastics such as Slug-Gos, Fin-S fish, and other jerk baits have found favor among surf fishermen, many of whom are switching to lighter rods so they can cast smaller, lighter offerings.

Anglers fishing from larger craft generally point their bows out toward the string of reefs and passages that connect Watch Hill Point to East Point at Fishers Island. When things are right, the fishing in this structure-rich area is as good as anyplace on the coast.

10

Watch Hill to Orient Point

Fishers Island, which is in New York waters (important when it comes to following fisheries regulations), lies diagonally in a west-southwesterly to north-northeasterly path that lines up with Little and Great Gull Islands, Plum Island, and Orient Point, New York. This entire run from Orient Point to Watch Hill holds some of the best striper and bluefish waters anywhere. This is also some of the most dangerous and treacherous water on the coast.

This entire zone is swept by strong currents and punctuated by islands, passages, and deep holes, with the underwater seascape between the visible landmarks just as erratic as a miniature underwater mountain range. This underwater structure kicks the fast-moving waters toward the surface over the reefs and humps to create dangerous and visible rip lines across all the reaches of open water from Long Island to Rhode Island. Currents that drain the Sound run at better than 5 knots at their peaks during moon tides. This, combined with the rock structure, is enough even to create visible whirlpools on the surface in the Race during the peak of outgoing tides. Strong currents keep the rock piles that rest on the bottom fairly clean, so snagged lines are a constant problem.

My son Jared when he was a little guy, on one of his first plug-casting trips for tunoids and bluefish off the Watch Hill Reef. Watch Hill Lighthouse is in the background.

The deepest water in this turbulent stretch is in the Race between Little Gull Island and Race Rock Light. It is the largest run of open water between Orient Point and Watch Hill. On maps it is officially called the Race.

It has maximum bottom depths ranging from 180 to 254 feet, in the passage between Race Rock Light and Valiant Rock. West of Valiant Rock—between there and Little Gull Island—is a second, narrower but deeper passage that runs 180 to 260 feet, with a 320-foot-deep hole half a mile or so on the seaward side of the rip lines themselves.

Between the Gull Islands and Plum Island is a shallow, 20- to 30-foot-deep shelf known as the Sluiceway that creates a wide zone of fast-moving water that always holds big bass, bluefish, and small tuna when they are present in the region. The waters almost boil over this shoal, creating some of the best striper habitat anywhere. In the middle of this turbulence, rising like a spire above the high tide, is a landmark called Old Silas Rock on the charts. Silas Rock has produced many of the 50-pound-plus bass caught in this part of the world over the years.

Watch Hill Point and Light. The reefs from here to Fishers Island create about 5 miles of absolutely excellent fishing for bass, bluefish, and false albacore in season.

When I first began striped bass fishing with more experienced friends, back in the late 1960s and early 1970s, we used to troll the Sluiceway. There were no GPS or loran units to guide us. The only way to navigate was to use a combination of compass courses and depth finder readings (on our old flasher unit), and dead reckoning with visible landmarks, or ranges. By triangulating visible shore points, it was possible to fish in approximately the same zones with some degree of accuracy.

We always fished by trolling wire-line rigs with 10-inch-long Gibbs Mackerel Plugs, Danny Plugs, or bucktail jigs tipped with pork rind strips. In those days, when the fish were in, tides were right, and the ranges could be seen, we loaded up with large striped bass ranging from 20 to 50 pounds with little trouble. That was before the striped bass disappearance in the late 1970s and early 1980s. Since the bass have rebounded, more of them are growing older and larger with every passing season, and this place is regaining the big-bass status it once held in the region.

Plum Gut, the 100-foot-deep cut between Plum Island and Orient Point, is a smaller version of the Race that may rip a tad faster due to the relatively smaller constriction. The Gut is actually the location where the Connecticut River's ancient channel has cut through the shelf for eons; it continues to be a drainage point for the waters of the Sound now that it has flooded completely since the glaciers.

A rip line sets up with the changing tides, creating a Race-like area of fast-moving, riled waters that hold and attract predatory fish such as bluefish and striped bass, which prey on the abundant bait that is pushed, pulled and often disoriented as it's drawn through this area of the Sound by passing tides. Predators take advantage of the fact that schools of bait are separated and therefore easier to pick off when tides are running strong.

A regional landmark, Race Rock Light is technically in New York State, but anglers from Connecticut consider it their own. The strong currents that build up in this area, as waters enter and leave Long Island Sound, create one of the best bass and bluefish fisheries anywhere in the country. Bring the Dramamine to fish this spot!

The result is a 22-mile string of islands, high spots, and deep passages between Long Island and the mainland that churn and boil with each changing tide, creating a habitat that attracts and holds all varieties of marine fish throughout the season. The Race, Plum Gut, and Watch Hill Reefs are three of the most heavily fished destinations in this part of the country. Why? Because they consistently produce excellent catches of bluefish, striped bass, and small tuna throughout the season. The calmer waters around their edges hold porgies, blackfish, and fluke in abundance, though most anglers who travel this far from shore tend to target the more glamorous, larger game-fish species. Bottom-dwelling species are generally targeted for the table or market, rather than sport, by anglers who fish closer to their home ports.

11

The Watch Hill/Fishers Island Reef Complex

Located just over the state line, the quaint seaside town of Watch Hill, Rhode Island, lies between two opposing points that jut out into the mouth of Long Island Sound. Watch Hill is a popular tourist and beachgoer destination, complete with pricey shops, restaurants, and their requisite heavy summer traffic. The town is easily reached via a 15-minute drive from exit 92 off I-95. Follow Route 2 into Westerly, pick up Route 1A, and follow it to Watch Hill by paying attention to the signs. All parking and main attractions are off the main drag through the center of town. Parking can be difficult—if not impossible—during vacation season.

During the off season or in the evenings, however, after the bulk of the tourists have gone home, it's possible park in a small lot across the road from the Watch Hill Lighthouse and walk to the rocks where all the fishing takes place. Watch Hill Light is a picturesque landmark as well as a famous angling destination that gives up some of the largest striped bass taken from the southern New England suds each year.

Surf fishermen like Watch Hill Light because the walk is very short and the fishing is usually more consistent than what's found at the end of the long walk to Napatree Point,

Sunset on the Watch Hill/Fishers Island Reef Complex, just off Catumb Rock with East Point, Fishers Island, in the background.

which can be a big disappointment if the fish aren't there. There is nearly always something to catch at either Watch Hill Point or Napatree Point; the problem is often reaching the fish, which may be feeding just out of casting range. Still, surf fishermen—especially those who stick it out through the night tides—take their share of jumbo bass after dark from the rugged, tide-swept Watch Hill Point and the back eddies on either side.

Most of the fish that come in from this area are caught from boats that string out along the numerous reefs and passages in the Watch Hill/Fishers Island Reef Complex or drift the sand-bottomed areas from there to Stonington for fluke. Numerous marinas and yacht clubs for boat moorages are located in and along the Pawcatuck River from Watch Hill to Westerly. A few of these private clubs or marinas have launches that nonmembers can pay to drop a boat in—though parking is often limited.

The best access to the entire area from the Mystic River through Stonington and east to Misquamicut Beach is the Barn Island State Launch in Stonington, just on the Connecticut side of the border. Get to Barn Island Launch by taking exit 91 off I-95, heading south down Main Street toward the borough of Stonington, taking a left (east) onto Route 1, turning right at the light for Greenhaven Road, crossing the small creek, then taking a quick right onto Palmer Neck Road. The launch is the end of this road, with parking for 65, though often 80 or more boats cram into the area by parking along the access road wherever it's possible to pull off the hardtop. This is a very popular launch that you must reach early on weekends or during off hours to be assured of a place to park and reasonable launch and pullout times.

Historically, anglers used to rent boats from small marinas in Stonington and the Pawcatuck River and start off the spring season fishing for winter flounder in Stonington Harbor, the Pawcatuck River, and Little Narragansett Bay. Later on, as the fish moved deep, flats could be caught in the hole off the outer breakwall at Stonington and out around Noyes Shoal before they dissipated out into the cooler, deeper waters of Long Island and Block Island Sounds.

Those days are long gone. Few, if any, anglers fish flounder anywhere in this area. At present, the sandy-bottomed zones in this region support a large fishery for fluke, which show up in the area feeding underneath the first schools of squid that move into the reefs sometime in May or early June.

From the time summer flounder arrive in the region each spring until they leave in fall (or at a season closure), armadas of boats set up in the various popular and productive drifts from White Rock, a mile or so west of Stonington, to Noyes Shoal (off the breakwalls); the channels around Stonington Harbor; Stonington Flats, from the breakwalls to Napatree Point's drop-off into deeper tide-swept waters; the crescent-shaped Watch Hill Beach; and the miles of sand beaches and shoals around the corner and north to Misquamicut Beach and beyond.

This entire stretch of water holds fluke all season long. These are all well-known fluke-fishing grounds within an easy boat ride of Barn Island Launch and any of the marinas in the area. Don't hesitate to take a contour map to help locate fluke drifts where you can float along some of the drop-offs, edges, and holes that punctuate the area. Fluke will inhabit any areas with the correct combination of bottom type (sand or gravel that is relatively clean and tide-swept) and food availability.

Fluke prefer to feed on squid and are nearly always found associated with concentrations of these cephalopods. They are also opportunists, however, and will often move into suprisingly shallow waters of 10 feet or less to take advantage of silversides, anchovies, sand eels, and juvenile menhaden when these are abundant and moving along the coast during late summer and fall.

In this area the shoals up inside the protection of Sandy Point often hold fishable numbers of fluke beginning sometime in August. Similar fisheries develop inside the mouths of the Mystic, Thames, Niantic, and other coastal rivers and embayments along the coast at the same time each year. These shallow-water inshore fisheries vary in intensity, timing, and location from year to year, depending on the distribution and abundance of the various forage sources that may develop in a given area. It's a matter of seeking them out when the juvenile herring and snapper blues show up, and dogging them from that time on.

As good as fluke fishing can be in the Watch Hill area, it's the string of reefs and rock piles between there and Fishers Island's East Point that attracts most of the angling attention throughout the year. The riled waters and fast currents set up rip lines that disorient bait, which in turn attracts schools of predatory species. This string of reefs is famous for the striped bass, bluefish, and (later in summer and fall) false albacore and bonito that are drawn to feed on whatever forage happens to be around.

Between Watch Hill Reef and Fishers Island lies a string of high reefs and passages that all hold fish when the bass and blues are around. Right at Watch Hill Light itself is Watch Hill Point. Extending a few hundred yards out into the crossing currents, it kicks up a wall of water that sometimes exceeds 5 feet when strong winds are blowing directly into the tides. At its end is Watch Hill Passage, the first break along this chain of bottom structure.

Beyond the passage is Watch Hill Reef, which is composed of three distinct high areas with smaller passages between. This is a prime zone for big bass, blues, and small tuna. Watch Hill Reef is followed by a larger break, Sugar Reef Passage, and then Sugar Reef—two distinct high points with a deeper U-shaped pocket between them. This pocket often holds and concentrates fish on the outgoing tide. Sugar Reef is marked by a distinct, tilted spire often decorated by cormorants sitting to dry their wings in the sun.

Farther west is Catumb Passage—the deepest trough that lets water out of the Sound in this string of reefs, with maximum depths reaching 50 feet or more. It lines up with the tip of Napatree Point so that waters flowing out from Fishers Island Sound through this gap have an unobstructed run, and have scoured this deep passage through eons of tidal changes.

Catumb Rock lies about midway between Watch Hill and Fishers Island. The rock itself is a Volkswagen-sized glacial erratic that lies just at or beneath the surface during high tide and above water on the ebb. It is located in the northern corner of this shallow, triangular-shaped shelf. Catumb Rocks can be a dangerous place. When large oceanic waves roll in from the Atlantic, they may curl up and break on this reef due to the sizable shallow shelf on top of this huge shallow pile of rocks; waves frequently build up and break *only* in this area when the seas are rough. When it's calm and waters clear, it's often possible to look down and see the kelp as you drift over the top of this reef. If your eyes are sharp you might see fish darting from under the shadow of the boat.

To the west are more high spots ranging from 12 to 18 feet deep in a narrow shelf leading from the red nun that marks one corner of Catumb Rocks to Lords Passage, the widest break in this reef complex. This passage runs anywhere from 29 to 40 feet deep.

Between Lords Passage and East Point, Fishers Island is the most significant abovewater structure in this string of rock piles. Wicopesset Island, a 100-yard-long, wave-pounded pile of rocks, creates a dangerous hazard to navigation; on the charts it looks like a left hand giving the thumb's-up signal with its pinkie extended. This shoal, which sits in a spot where it is often pounded by big surf from the Atlantic and swept clean by strong currents on all sides, it is a veritable striper hot spot that has given up many of the bona fide 50-even 60-pound striped bass caught in this part of the world over the years.

Wicopessett Island is one of those areas that will give up smaller stripers to anglers tossing soft plastics, shallow swimmers, or poppers, while those fishing with live bait are setting the steel to fish over 20 pounds.

Due to the strong currents that blow through these passages, there are times during the season when the bait moves out, taking the gamefish with it. As a result you'll experience short periods of time just about every year when the reefs off Watch Hill are nearly barren and hardly worth fishing. A thorough pass over prime spots with a fish finder will yield a few marks from resident blackfish and an occasional stray bass, but that's it—not enough life to support any sort of major fishing activities. When this happens simply look elsewhere—in the Sound, along the south shore beaches, or around Fishers Island—because the fish seldom move very far from this hotbed of activity.

The typical seasonal progression off the Watch Hill Reef Complex begins in late May or early June, when an inshore movement of spawning squid draws and concentrates the stripers that are migrating through the area at that time. During this "squid bite" (as I like to call it), bass are scattered throughout the region, feeding on everything from alewives in coastal rivers to squid off the reefs. The abundance of squid concentrates stripers off these reefs as well as in the Race, leading off the opposite end of Fishers Island.

The squid bite, like many natural events, is relatively shortlived. The fishing may begin to build one weekend, peak the next, and be pretty well shot by the third. The peak of the squid bite is marked by fishing that includes large to average-sized fish in the 28- to 35-inch range, with a smattering of larger fish being caught by anglers throwing artificial lures and flies on or near the surface when stripers are concentrated and actively feeding during tide changes. During the same time period, anglers fishing the reefs after dark with rigged fresh squid, live eels, or chunk baits sunk down deep with sinkers and lead-core or wire lines take even larger fish. It's a great time to be on the water.

Anglers using artificials will obviously do best with lures that mimic squid. Yozuri Hydro Squirts are perhaps the best clone around at the moment, and they have accounted for some humongous bass since they hit the market in 2001. Just as deadly in the rips when the bass are slurping squid from the rip lines are 6- and 9-inch Slug-Gos, large white or light-colored tube jigs, and molded soft plastic squid clones such as those made by McKala or Luhr Jensen in 3- to 5-inch sizes. These large soft plastic squid lures are excellent matches for this particular bite and can be fished Carolina style: 2 or 3 feet behind a sinker, on a plain hook, and cast like any lure or on a jighead, depending on how deep the fish are. All it takes is an influx of squid and the proper water temperatures.

Of course the classic white or chartreuse bucktail with a pork rind or Mario's Plastic Squid strip as a teaser will take bass due to its natural squidlike appearance. However, the soft plastics rigged without additional weight sink more slowly and have a more natural floating action when drifting or being retrieved in the water column. For this reason, they usually catch more stripers, especially when the fish are feeding on or within 10 feet of the surface. Use classic jigs or weighted soft plastic squids when they are deeper and not visibly feeding in the rip, but are marking on the fish finder screen.

Look for the stripers and blues to concentrate on the down-tide side of reefs during tidal changes. This means that during a flood tide, when the water is flowing from east to west as it enters the Sound in this area, fish on the western edge or in the passages between high spots along the reefs. When the tide ebbs, switch sides and concentrate on the east or opposite side of the reefs. There will often be fish clustered on both sides of reefs and surface rocks during the tides. Still, more of them will be in the lee of the current, rather than up front and fighting it, unless they are feeding on top, in the rip lines themselves. This is often the case during the spring squid bite.

I lost one of the largest stripers I've ever hooked on an artificial lure on the lee side of this rock pile during the spring squid bite. I couldn't even begin to slow this monster down as it swam from the rocks right past the bow of my boat and down through some boulders, where it broke off. I saw this behemoth in the clear water of spring. It was close to, if not over 50 pounds. Unfortunately I was light-tackle fishing and targeting schoolies when it struck a big Slug-Go; I was woefully under-gunned with my 10-pound-test line and a medium-action 6½-foot spinning rod.

Immediately after the squid bite, some of the bass move north, especially during summers when temperatures heat to a boil early in June and July. During cooler, wetter summers, however, many of the stripers remain in this area, where they provide a steady, quality fishery that tapers off slowly, rather than dropping off rapidly to near nothing during the latter part of summer.

As summer settles in you may find some of those slow-to-dead periods, especially during early August, as various food sources move into and through this tide-swept area. Still, there are nearly always a few big bass spending the summer around the Watch Hill Reef Complex and are there to do battle just about any evening after dark.

During this time frame, sportfishermen and commercial pin hookers work the reefs most successfully with live baits such as hickory shad, menhaden (if any can be captured), and live eels. These baits may be drifted or worked deep along the bottom and edges of the passages, using three-way swivels and sinkers that may need to be 8 to 16 ounces in order to hold the bottom. This method isn't as much fun as free-lining, but it's often more effective reaching the larger stripers on a regular basis.

Sometime during July the "after-work bites" begin to develop here as elsewhere in the region. This is the phenomenon that occurs when there are large concentrations of small baitfish in the area. Bluefish and striped bass, though they may be catchable all day long, seem to concentrate and push baits to the surface, where visible blitzes take place on a daily, or rather "eveningly" basis. Not to say fish won't come up top at any time, but this dusk and (often) dawn bite is an event that sportfishers can count on for some fun.

The majority of summertime catches are usually run-of-the-mill schoolie bass and bluefish of whatever size happens to be prevalent at the time. Success amounts to running a paper route from place to place in order to capitalize on any fish that may be popping on the surface. Despite the fact that stripers and blues are probably present and feeding down deep, these visible surface blitzes are not only fun fishing, but also easy. There is no doubt where the fish are and where lures or flies should be cast. While fish are blasting around and feeding on the surface, the odds of drawing a strike are high—as are the thrills. Many anglers choose to cruise the reefs and nearby shorelines, glassing key areas and casting blind to others, in the hope of being in the right place at the right time. On most late-summer and early-fall evenings they will not be disappointed.

When the fishing becomes difficult and the easy surface blitzes do not develop as expected, there are other options. Trolling with swimming plugs or baits can be effective. A sure-fire way of deskunking yourself when easy fish can't be located—beginning in late spring after the first bass arrive in the area, and continuing until the last one heads south in fall—is tube and worm trolling, a simple method of taking bass that is both easy and very effective.

Tube trollers sink garden-hose-like tubes baited with the largest whole sandworms available down to the bottom around the edges of reefs using lead-core or wire line. The other, more fun option is to troll smaller tubes baited with whole sandworms or Berkley Power Sand Worms on a flat line from a medium to light spinning or bait-casting rod with 20- to 30-pound Fireline as close to the shoreline rocks (literally anywhere) as possible. Go dead slow—1½ to 2 miles per hour, in 6 to 12 feet of water—and hold on.

During mid-August the anglers who cruise the reefs in search of those evening blitzes begin looking for the telltale fast-moving, hard-to-catch schools of bonito and false albacore that move inshore once water temperatures reach their seasonal maximum.

The Watch Hill end of the Watch Hill/Fishers Island Reef Complex is where most of the action takes place from small tuna. This is logical due to the fact that these fish are generally ripping up or down the coast, pursuing baitfish along Rhody's south shore beaches or the Connecticut shoreline; thus they pass through the gap at the mouth of the Sound more often closer to the mainland side. For this reason, when you're looking for these often hard-to-catch fish, start at Watch Hill Light and search out along the reefs or shoreline in the direction of the prevailing tides from there. These speedsters will often run up and down the chain of reefs between the light and East Point, holding for part of a tide then vanishing, only to show up a mile or so downtide, where people often suffer through a few minutes of angling frustration. The small tuna are often very hard to hook.

Generally speaking, on an incoming tide the small tuna push through the reefs after holding for a quick snack for a time span ranging from a couple of casts to most of a tide, depending on bait availability. Then they swoop either along the north side of Fishers Island or along the Connecticut coast, settling in for short periods off the Mystic River at Bluff Point in Groton, often ending up at the mouth of the Thames River, off Pleasure Beach in Waterford, or the Millstone Outflow and Niantic Bay.

During good tuna years, schools of these fish simultaneously move into the Sound through the Race, Sluiceway, and Plum Gut, creating fisheries as far west as Guilford and Madison. Occasionally tunas and their cousins, including Spanish mackerel, briefly show up as far west as Penfield Reef. The majority of sightings and catches of bonito and false albacore, however, take place from Niantic Bay to the east and around Fishers Island.

Though anglers look for them off "the reefs" every year, some years are hot and some years aren't. Generally the best angling occurs in warm summers with an abundance of sand eels, silversides, butterfish, juvenile menhaden, and anchovies in the waters of eastern Long Island Sound—the conditions necessary to attract and hold tuna from August through October. In cool, wet summers or if sufficient bait is not present, they may show up sporadically for a couple of weeks, frustrating the anglers who have waited all season for a shot at them. They are usually difficult to locate and hook because they move so rapidly. When they do settle into an area to feed—say, the Millstone Point Outflow—it is easier (but never easy) to hook up and do battle. For this reason the Watch Hill Reef area can be very good for bonito and falsies when conditions are right and lousy when they aren't.

Fly fishermen often shine when the albies are present, because the slow, hanging action of flies perfectly mimics many of the small baits they are feeding on. Bonito are much more selective in what they take for lures. This species usually likes baits to be small and fast moving. False albacore are more aggressive and are known to take small hard-swimming plugs and even poppers on occasion.

The best lures for taking either species must be small and should generally have a narrow profile. When butterfish and juvenile menhaden are the prime food source, however, Yozuri Rattlin' Vibes, Rattling Raps, Rat-L-Traps, and similar lures in silver or natural shad colors can be effective. The most popular tuna lures are small, long-casting, sliver-shaped spoons such as Deadly Dicks, Kastmasters, Needle Eels, and others. Spoons are the best choice when fishing for albies from shore because they cast so well; they can increase the odds of hooking a fish simply because during the course of a trip they will cover more ground.

When the gamefish are chasing narrow-profile baits such as sand eels, silversides, baby bunker, or mummichogs, small-sized soft plastics such as Slug-Gos, Fin-S fish, Living Eye Minnows, and the new small-sized Salt Shakers will all work well. For some reason, friends and I have had excellent success over the years catching false albacore on 5½-inch Mambo Minnows in green and chrome colors. Small suspending swimmers such as Husky Jerks and Rebel swimmers also take fish. Once or twice when albies were marking under the boat but not hitting other more shallow-running lures, they have succumbed to short, narrow-profile deep divers such as Spoonbill Rebels and Bomber Deep A's run down to them either by casting or trolling.

Even in the good years, when conditions are prime, the small tuna move about so rapidly and are so picky when it comes to taking lures that they are usually more of a frustration to anglers than anything. Yet they are such hard fighters, capable of dumping many yards of line off a light spinning or fly reel, that a growing legion waits patiently for them each summer, and takes up the challenge these little bullets bring to the eastern Long Island Sound fishing menu almost every season.

The deep, tide-swept reefs between the mainland and Fishers Island also hold some huge blackfish (tautog) and monstrous humpback porgies. I accidentally caught my largest scup, a dinner-plate-sized near-3-pounder, back in the mid-1980s on a whole live squid that was meant for a striped bass. When bass fishing, the fish finder is constantly marking decent-sized blackfish and schools of scup that are hugging to the rocks along the faces and drop-offs in this reef complex. Unfortunately the currents are so strong in this area that it's difficult to effectively fish for these two bottom-hugging species. Thus all but a few commercial pin hookers targeting jumbo porgies fish inshore, where the waters are friendlier.

Deep tube trolling, chunk fishing off wire or lead-core line, sinking rigged squid back to the passages, and drifting eels over and around the reefs from dusk through dawn generally account for most of the jumbo bass brought to the scales every season. The smaller blues and bass are usually scratched off the surface by fly fishermen and light-tackle spin casters who toss poppers, swimming diving lures, or soft plastics that match the prevailing forage. By being diversified in your approach to fishing this terrific stretch of water, it's usually possible to find something to do battle with at any time during the season—but not always.

12

Fishers Island Proper

Fishers Island is part of New York State, despite the fact it's much closer to both Connecticut and Rhode Island. It was originally owned by Governor Winthrop of Connecticut. He bought it and turned it into a farm where he raised goats, cows, and horses. Then the Duke of York laid claim to the island—a dispute that wasn't settled until 1664, when a joint committee from both states assigned it as a territory of New York. Around that time the farm, which the Winthrops had sold, was broken up into smaller plots. A couple of the landowners developed their lands as a hunting preserve and stocked the island with pheasant, quail, and other gamebirds. As time went on the partitioning became greater, eventually evolving into the exclusive residential community that it is today. Now the island sports three golf courses, limited sport hunting, and some great fishing for those who own the oceanfront parcels, but little in the way of public access.

The legacy of the game clubs lives on in a naturally reproducing resident wild pheasant population. Anglers are often treated to their crowing early and late in the day as they fish along to the island's rocky shoreline. One memorable striper trip to the south side of the island was topped off by a 40-inch striper, which was applauded by a crowing cock bird on a patch of bright green lawn around the "castle" at East Point, like some medieval scene. It was one of those fishing trips that I will always remember as much for its the setting as for my catch.

Unlike other prime striped bass surf-fishing destinations, such as Block Island or Martha's Vineyard, Fishers Island is owned by a small number of very rich people who do not want anyone else there. No efforts are made to promote tourism; in fact, the contrary is more like it. As a result, there minimal shops and services, no bike or scooter rentals, and only one small hotel; it's even tough to get a cab ride in this place. Fishers Island's shoreline is under private ownership, with huge parcels of land separating each incredible shorefront home, beach club, or golf course. Essentially it is closed off to the public—period.

Jared Sampson with a 31-pounder taken on tube and worm off Fishers Island. Fish like this and bigger are caught regularly here or off the major rips of the Race and Fishers Island/Watch Hill Reef Complex.

One pain-in-the-neck—yet possible!—option open to surf-fishing anglers would be to take the Fishers Island ferry out of New London, then walk a short distance south out to tide-swept rocks at Race Point and fish in the surf. The other option is to make a short run in a private boat or with a charter captain and enjoy the great fishing and scenic vistas.

This forced seclusion is one reason Fishers Island is not as famous for striped bass fishing as the other island "striper meccas." Anyone who has ever fished its coastline knows that every inch is absolutely beautiful striped bass habitat. Other than inside a couple of very shallow, dangerously rocky coves, over the years I have caught stripers, many decent-sized stripers, from every hundred-yard stretch of this island's perimeter. Some spots are so productive my buddies and I have labeled individual rocks (which wouldn't show up on a map) with handles like Big Fish Rock, Big Fish Rock II, Miserable Rock, No Name Rock, and others that can't be printed here.

The island is roughly 7 miles long and 1 mile across at its widest point. It lies at a slight northeast–southwest angle across the mouth of Long Island Sound, roughly a third of the way across the gap from Watch Hill, Rhode Island. When the tides are running, water sweeps along both sides of the island, carrying bait and pursuing gamesters with every change in direction.

Sometimes fish are scattered along the shores; at other times they're clumped up in schools chasing the bait. For this reason, if a favorite fishing hole does not give up a fish or at least some sign of the presence of fish, keep moving until you make contact.

One of the good things about having such a large island with so much shoreline to cover is that if one place is being worked by another boat, there are hundreds of other great spots to wet a line. Granted, like everywhere else, there are some true hot spots that always seem to hold bass and blues, including both ends of the island. Race Point—which runs out into the riled, fast-running waters of the Race—and East Point, with the fishy Wicopesset Passage along its rocky end, are nothing short of phenomenal areas to catch stripers and bluefish.

Winds are always a factor around the island. Anglers who get blown out of the Race or the reefs can generally find quality striper waters in lee of the wind by simply heading to one of the protected shorelines of Fishers Island. Due to the island's stretched-out diamond shape, there is almost always a comparatively calm place out of strong winds somewhere along the rocky shore to troll, cast, or drift an eel.

There are times when it is dangerous or simply too rough to fish effectively here, especially on the south side, which is exposed directly to the Atlantic. Often the slightly cooler waters on the south side of Fishers, which are a longer run from the mainland and therefore more lightly fished, seems to produce many of the larger striped bass caught outside the Race and reefs every season. But stay away when the wind is blowing hard off the ocean and ground swells are making people ill, or crashing on the rocks, making it too tricky to work the shoreline. Instead simply hook up and run to the protected "inside," where there are plenty of excellent rock piles, ledges, and dropoffs to work.

Fishers Island is a great destination for any type of fishing. Granted, it's best suited for catching striped bass and bluefish, but its shorelines also offer beautiful habitat and therefore large numbers of blackfish and porgies, while its deep-water sandy reaches are some of the region's hottest fluke drifts. Later in the summer there are always some false albacore or bonito ripping around within striking distance of its rocky shore or off either of its tide-swept ends. When it's hot, oddball catches such as king mackerel, cobia, jack crevalle, and Spanish mackerel have been reported.

Due to the area's direct exposure to the Atlantic, occasional sharks have been seen or hooked in along the shore or out in the Race. Historically, there have been sightings, hookups, and even limited catches of medium and giant bluefin tuna in the Race. In fact, back in the 1960s and 1970s members of the New London Tuna Club used to make a run to a shoal between Fishers Island and Block Island called "Rosie's Ledge" that was a little-known but documented giant bluefin tuna ground.

Perhaps the most consistently productive fishing spot on the island—from both shore and boat—is Race Point. My dad used to travel to Fishers Island on the ferry with a friend. Actually, he was dragged there by that friend, with whom he would walk to Race Point and fish the night tides. He liked the trip, because he usually caught fish—he wasn't a very skilled angler, so it must be a bona fide hot spot.

I have never cast a plug from shore, but I've drifted within a short distance of the island at Race Point countless times over the years. It's one of those "litmus test" sort of places. If you approach the string of large boulders that run out toward the green buoy and Race Rock Lighthouse when the tide is running strong, make a dozen casts, and don't get a bite—go home, don't waste your time, because there are no fish around.

The best fishing at Race Point will occur during the ebb tide, though many times the bass tuck in on the north side of the point, in along the rocks during the flood tide, providing a constant stream of action as long as the water is flowing hard over this shoal. Often the gulls work over the top of surface-feeding stripers and bluefish around Race Point, particularly during late summer and early fall, but the birds are not always there to provide guidance; often they are out working the edges of the rip lines of the Race.

This place is always worth fishing with small swimming plugs, soft plastics, poppers, flies, and speed jigs. Even when it's slow, it's often possible to catch that initial, sometimes hard-to-find deskunker from these rocks.

After the sun goes down, the string of rocks and reef leading off Race Point is a great spot to drift with live eels. Simply run up into the tide, as close to the visible rocks as possible. Cut the engine, sling a live eel (with no additional weight or, at most, a small slip or peg sinker) right up to the side of the largest visible boulders, and drift it back with the tide. On an outgoing tide, which will sweep along the island's shallow waters, the drift can be a few hundred yards before the waters drop off to 20 feet or more, making the weightless eel less effective. Reel up and repeat the process.

Among my fishing buddies, the largest bass any of us officially weighed, a fat 48-pounder, was caught drifting with eels at Race Point as described above. Over the years this technique has provided us with many thrilling hookups from huge striped bass. Bluefish can be a problem here, so don't sacrifice too many eels before switching to artificials or moving to another place.

It's not a good idea to anchor up here. This is partly because other anglers may want to fish, and it's not right to hog such a great spot with a single boat, and partly because the rocks and strong tides sometimes make it difficult to free anchors. Smaller boats have on occasion been sunk when the waves kicked up and they were tethered to the bottom in the strong currents that sweep this area.

One reason Fishers Island itself is such a great and relatively easy place to fish for striped bass is the fact that it has a narrow shelf comprised of beach sands, cobble, boulders, or a combination of all three, which drops off into deeper waters of 20 to 40 feet. This constant access to deep water means big bass can and often are literally anywhere along the perimeter of the island.

The best approach for fishing is to run from point to point, giving special attention to the larger rocks and reefs. Running the south or outer side of Fishers Island, anglers typically set up a paper route, hitting all their favorite spots. The major landmarks that show up on most charts are places such as Wilderness Point, Isabella Beach, Schooner Reef, Gatanby Rock, Barley Field Cove, Wreck Island, and East Point. All the great-looking minor points, coves, and rock piles in between these landmark fishing holes will hold stripers and or blues, as will any other location along this superfishy shoreline.

Simmon's Castle, a landmark at East Point, Fishers Island. I caught my personal best bass in front of this incredible structure, a 44-pounder on a live eel. Many much bigger bass have been caught within the space shown in this picture, and nearby Wicopesset Passage and Island.

Of the lot, Wilderness Point probably accounts for the most big bass every season. This long, sweeping point has one of the steeper drop-off gradients along this side of the island and is therefore a magnet for larger stripers. The tip of Wilderness Point, where it curves in to meet the western edge of Isabella Beach, is a particularly hot spot that you should always hit with whatever bait or lure is on your rod at the time. It is perhaps best suited for eel fishing after dark, but we've taken many stripers from 35 to 45 inches on tube and worm rigs from this place, along with a smattering of jumbos that fell to artificial lures.

These same rocky points that hold stripers are also great porgy and blackfish producers. Most anglers don't travel the long distance to Fishers Island to catch these species, but they are usually available if the bass or fluke are not cooperating. Wilderness Point and the rocks off Barley Field Cove are also great scup-fishing zones that often produce fish in the 2- to 3-pound class later in the season.

Blackfish are everywhere. When we were teenagers and more hardy, or foolhardy, we never fished for blackfish, opting instead to jump in the water anywhere along Fishers Island's rock-strewn perimeter with a spear gun or Hawaiian sling and shoot what we wanted. Unless visibility was horrid, it was easy. At present, despite the fact blackfish numbers have dropped considerably in the three decades since my spear-fishing days, there are still loads of blackfish here. I know, because I often see them in the clear water while maneuvering the boat around the rocks to troll tube and worms.

The entire south side of Fishers Island holds some fluke, often big ones. It is one of the major fluke-fishing destinations in the eastern third of Connecticut and southern Rhode Island. During outgoing tides, there are backwashes off both tips of the island at Race Point, and at East Point, where you can drift successfully for fluke.

The shallow shelf is a bit wider and shallower in front of the airfield near Race Point where it runs over to Wilderness Point. This stretch is a fairly productive fluke drift. Depending on water temperatures, we have caught fish anywhere from 10 to 40 feet deep in this area.

The most popular fluke drift on the island is out in front of Isabella Beach on either side of the strip of lobster pot buoys in that area, and off Schooner Reef, in waters ranging from 20 to 70 feet deep. (Don't give in to temptation and touch a pot; lobstermen and conservation officers don't take kindly to lobster thieves. Give the pots some space when drifting for this reason, and to minimize the odds of leaving a rig on their buoy lines.) I've had good success fluke fishing east of there by drifting from deep water up into the numerous small pockets and coves that stretch along the shoreline. The best drifts will be just on the sandy side of rock piles wherever you happen to be fishing. By running near groups of lobster pots, which provide a constant fish-attracting chum slick and on up inside or against the beaches until it gets too bony or shallow, we have taken some nice catches of fluke over the years. Later on the summer flounder may be as shallow as 10 to 15 feet in these places, especially when they are in tight and feeding on peanut bunker or juvenile butterfish.

The drift from outside Wreck Island, in 35 to 45 feet of water, east to the hole scoured out by the waters raging through Wicopesset Passage is another prime fluke spot, with the emphasis on taking big doormats. The biggest fluke I've ever lost hit a whole squid drifted at the end of the ebb tide, just before it went slack, in 40 to 75 feet of water, directly in front of and half a mile out from the gap between Wicopesset Island and East Point. It's a tough spot to fish, but worth a shot for a big fish at the end of either tide when action slacks off in adjacent areas.

The inside of Fishers Island—because it is protected and out of the strong sweeping tides and waves of the Atlantic—has more character in the form of coves and inlets. Everything here is edged with rocks, making nearly all of it good-to-excellent striper water. Again, the best fishing zones will be where the shelf drops off more quickly to deep water. The big ones will hold here during the day to get out of the bright sunlight.

I haven't tried it in years, due to the lack of winter flounder throughout the region in general, but a couple of decades back, before this species was wiped out by commercial overharvest, we used to fish the shallow 20-foot waters leading into West Harbor during June and have pretty good success on a mixed bag of both winter and summer flounder, with some porgies and blackfish mixed in when the boat drifted near the rocks.

Few anglers fish this area at all, but it must still be a pretty good fluke drift, especially on those days when the wind is blowing hard out of the south or east. West Harbor, plus the shoals around nearby Flat Hammock Island and South Dumpling, is a protected area that is worth testing out for fluke anytime, but especially when winds are howling and a calm refuge is needed.

It is also possible to drift for fluke inside the East, Middle, and West Clumps, which are rock piles that reach the water's surface about a quarter mile off the north side of Fishers Island. Few anglers do it, but it is possible to find some open fluke drifts between the clumps and the shoreline of the island. At times out-of-the-way, lightly fished areas along the "inside" of the island may be productive for this reason. As the summer progresses, fluke are often picked over by draggers and rod-and-reelers, reducing the average catch in both size and number. For this reason, in later summer it's often worthwhile to break the regime and seek out new, little-known drifts in out-of-the-way places such as the north side of the island, in Fishers Island Sound.

The steep drop-offs into deep water from rocky shorelines from North Hill to Race Point, and around North Dumpling, provide popular and productive fishing for anglers targeting porgies.

While most of the boat traffic coming from the mainland bypasses the excellent fishing grounds along the north shore of the island in favor of the rough but very productive waters of the Race, these spots make a great striper-fishing alternative.

Most years, the largest striper that is caught on my boat comes out of the Race or off Wilderness Point, places with exposure to the open Atlantic. Still, very often the runners-up are taken by fishing eels or tube and worm rigs between Race Point and North Hill on the western tip of the island, or from East Point to Brooks Point at the eastern end. My wife Karen's best striper, a 43″, 35-pounder, was caught on a tube-and-worm rig trolled inside the island.

My wife Karen with a 35-pound striper, her biggest, taken in the north or "inside" of Fishers Island while tube-and-worm trolling with a light-tackle spinning rod and 20-pound-test Fireline.

Bluefish turn up in the mix, with striped bass more frequent as the summer progresses, especially when fishing around Race Point or along the south side of Fishers Island. It's the same with the bonito and false albacore that show up in August. The "falsies" and "bonnies" can usually be found, when the tides are ripping, somewhere along a large, flounder-hook-shaped loop starting at Silver Eel Cove (the ferry slip) around Race Point and all the way to Watch Hill. It's a matter of running the route and looking for their telltale surface forays along the way.

Small tuna can be readily identified when blitzing on the surface, because they don't swirl when they take a bait like bluefish or striped bass do, making what I call a "toilet flush" boil. Instead they crash the surface in a linear fashion at great speeds, with their telltale blade-shaped fins or tails often visible as they cut the surface like a knife, then zip back down into the water column. The action is usually best when the turn of a tide coincides with dawn or dusk. Most anglers run the Watch Hill Reef Complex, then run the back of the island to Race Point and out into the Race, possibly as far as the Sluiceway, if need be, when looking for surface action from small tuna. This is a good tactic for those after-work summer trips that run from late afternoon until dark. Run-and-gun tactics will usually bring an encounter with some species of surface-feeding fish that could be mixed bass and blues, or small tuna with bass and blues feeding around the edges. It's all a matter of bait availability, weather, water temps, and luck.

13

The Race, Gull Islands, the Sluiceway, Plum Island, and Plum Gut

Though not technically in Connecticut waters, the Race to Little and Great Gull Islands, the shallow, riled shelf named the Sluiceway, Plum Island's perimeter, and Plum Gut, the third deep break that lets water out of Long Island Sound, are all within a reasonable ride for Connecticut anglers with seaworthy craft. In fact, these places are fished as much by Connecticut boats as those with New York registrations, particularly in the waters east of the Sluiceway.

The Race is classic deep-water bluefish and striped bass habitat at its riled best. By far it is the most heavily fished area in the region. The Race draws any and all anglers with a boat that is high-sided and sturdy enough to take its dangerous rip line and strong currents. There isn't a serious saltwater fisherman I know who hasn't fished the Race at least once. Sometimes once is enough, because it is a miserable, rough stretch of water.

Very rarely some hard-core blackfish and porgy fishermen squeak in to drop a line during slack-tide periods around Race Rock Light or Race Point, but these waters are really the home of the big boys. A scup swimming around the base of the lighthouse is more likely to be eaten by a big bass or blue than not. In fact, before large minimum length limits were imposed on scup, friends and I would sometimes stop at North Hill and catch a dozen small ones to use as hook baits when the tackle shop ran out of eels. They worked just fine.

The Race is relatively devoid of life, other than lobsters in its depths, until the month of May. Historically, anglers used to fish the Race and waters of that area on out to Wilderness Point for mackerel, pollack, and even some cod around its edges during April and early May, switching over to the stripers when they showed up later in the month, and bluefish once they entered its waters a month after that.

The pollack, a cold-water species, has disappeared from these waters due to the increased water temps and heavy overharvest in their core waters to the north. As northern populations shrank, the fish seemed to pull back to the epicenter of their home range and leave the fringe waters of the Race and similar areas to the south by the late 1970s.

The mackerel fishery lingered a tad longer but ultimately followed the pollack, dying out by the early 1980s. Atlantic mackerel used to enter Long Island Sound for two or three weeks each spring to spawn, and still do to a barely noticeable degree. During the hot decade of the 1980s, they apparently began bypassing the relatively warm waters of Long Island Sound in favor of the cooler temps found from Cape Cod and to the north. Despite a return to more normal temperatures recently, the macks have not returned in force. Occasionally, since their disappearance, there have been mackerel forays into the Sound by small schools of these fish, and during late summer and fall "tinker mackerel" show up and are gobbled down by bluefish and striped bass in the waters of the Race, around Fishers Island, and in eastern Long Island Sound. Unfortunately, what was once a mainstay seasonal fishery has been pretty much eliminated from the region's fishing menu since the early 1980s. Mackerel are still caught along the Rhode Island coast and Block Island; they just don't seem to like the Sound anymore.

The Race, Sluiceway, and Plum Gut are basically striper and bluefish waters that require a seaworthy boat, heavy tackle, and strong intestinal fortitude to fish. They're classic seasick waters. Most of the fishermen who work these areas usually use 30- or 50-pound-test line on heavy boat rods. Some use the heaviest superlines that match their tackle. Heavy breaking strength is required, more for its ability to handle heavy (16–20 ounce) weights and lures required to reach bottom or straighten hooks or otherwise pull loose from the countless bottom snags in these areas than to play the big bass it holds.

There are three basic ways to attack these waters: fishing deep, through or at specific depths within the water column, and on or within 10 feet of the surface. Use the depth finder to determine where the fish are and target them.

Most of the bluefish and jumbo bass taken from the Race are caught by anglers fishing deep with baited drail or three-way rigs with jigs or bait. Eels are the easiest live bait to get. Live porgies, snapper bluefish, hickory shad, and menhaden will also take some big bass from the depths of the Race. The key is using enough weight to get the bait or lure down to within a couple of feet of the bottom. Fish insufficient weight, and the offerings will be lifted up off the bottom and well out of the zone, where most of the fish will be holding, by its fast-flowing waters.

When fish are suspended midway in the water column, it's possible to send these same rigs down to the appropriate depth by using a spread of your arms as a measuring stick; this equals about 5 feet. It's simplest to determine what depth the fish are swimming at, then figure two "wingspans" for every 10 feet they are down from the surface.

Bluefish will often work up and down through the water column when feeding, occasionally making it tricky to reach them. An old-style way of taking these fish is a method known as "sqidding." This technique was originated by handliners, who would drop a heavy metal jig to the bottom and haul it up as fast as possible. All you have to do is hit the bottom and reel like crazy. In a current the jig will zig-zag up toward the surface at a sharp angle, like a squid trying to escape. This is a workout with the old 2:1 level winds, but it's a snap with a high-speed reel.

Count the cranks on the reel handle while reeling the lure up from the bottom, and note the number of cranks where strikes occur. This gives you the depth where the fish and lure are on the same plane. Reel to that point, then focus on this depth by reeling a few more cranks and dropping back down a few times, rather than bringing the lure all the way to the surface every time. This trick gives the lure a yo-yo effect as it is dragged by the drifting boat into the rips. Squidding is also effective on bluefish that are rapidly moving around while feeding somewhere in the middle of the water column.

Moderate depths to about 50 feet can also be worked effectively by trolling. Most marine anglers do not use downriggers, but a big cannonball is a great way to send smaller artificial offerings down deep where the bigger fish are holding. Most private and charter boats troll, or "snap," wire or leadcore lines. The method is simple.

Lines are set 150 to 200 feet back behind the boat; with wire, this will sink 20 to 25 feet with a jig, shallower with a swimming plug. The captain maneuvers the boat just outside the rip line, so the strong current pulls the offering into the edge of the breaking water where most of the bass and blues are concentrated. This works well near the surface or down as deep as the limitations of this style of gear allow. The boat is then run along the front of the rip line, alternately moving forward, dropping back with the current, and pulling ahead again with the motors. It is perhaps the most effective and efficient method of covering the edge of the rip line, one that is much more comfortable than being dragged into the slop while bottom bouncing.

Fishing the surface is usually matter of casting under birds or to visible breaks with poppers, shallow swimmers, big streamer flies, Slug-Go jerk baits, or soft plastic cranking jigs.

The best, most reliable surface bites of the season set up in the Race around the same time they do off the Watch Hill Reefs—sometime between late June and early July—and continue right through fall, when the blitzes may go on nonstop for an entire tide, die off at slack water, then pick back up once the tide begins moving in the other direction.

In late summer false albacore or bonito may be caught anywhere in the Race, but they tend to show and hold most frequently at either end, near Race Point or from Little Gull Island on the shoals of the Sluiceway.

The Sluiceway is just far enough out of the way for most anglers that it does not see anywhere near the amount of pressure as the Race and nearby Plum Gut. This means that when the albies are present, there will be fewer idiots around to run them over and put them down. If tuna aren't around, drop a lure or bait for a big striper.

As a budding young angler, the first monster 40-pound-plus stripers I ever saw caught came from the Sluiceway. This was in the days when mackerel were a forage species that was abundant in spring and present in smaller numbers throughout summer. You could catch one anytime and live-line it off a deep-water reef; it was as close to a guaranteed big bass as you can get.

When live mackerel weren't available, I used big Gibbs Mackerel Plugs—classic striped bass swimmers that look like the lower 10 inches of a baseball bat, with a mackerel paint job and metal lips to make them dive and wiggle.

In those days of flashers and "ranges," the guy I fished with would line up two points of land, find the 20-foot contour, and set back 125 feet of wire; as an angler all I did was hold on. The boat and stripers did the rest. It was easy big-bass fishing at its finest. The only bad thing about it was the heavy, clunky gear that was the norm in those days, which took away from the fun of fighting these big bruisers.

To this day anglers still run out to the Sluiceway and drift over it with a live menhaden or hickory shad that is sunk to the bottom in its rocky, rugged, riled, 20- to 30-foot depths. The same thing can be done with live eels and deep-diving plugs. Today, just like back in the 1970s, many fishermen run up to Silas Rock, toss a live eel to this classic, columnlike piece of granite, and hook into bruiser-sized stripers.

The bass fishing tends to be better around Silas Rock and the deeper waters closer to Plum Island, while bluefish and false albacore tend to bunch up and hold in the narrow, 10-foot-deep shoals extending off the west end of Great Gull Island. Late summer and fall is the time to plug this productive little stretch of subsurface real estate.

The shores of Plum Island are great fishing, but be sure you don't set foot on this piece of "verboten" government land. This small island is a government animal disease research center, or so we are told. The signs alongshore spell out the fact that under no circumstances is anyone to set foot here. For this reason alone, most fishermen stay well away—you never know what may be blowing in the wind.

On the south side of Plum Island are some excellent rocky shoals that are prime tube and worm trolling or nighttime shallow eel-casting habitat. It's a wide, shallow, boulder-strewn shelf. Where this shelf drops off into a 120-foot hole that is blown out by the tides ripping through Plum Gut, it's sometimes possible to take some decent fluke—though again, this area is primarily reserved by anglers for chasing stripers and bluefish.

Most of the fish along the visible rip lines throughout this fishy stretch of water will be on the front side of the standing waves, whether you are casting on the surface or bouncing a drail rig along the bottom. Be sure the lure or bait is working at the desired depth when you encounter the zone within 100 feet or so of the rip line. Deep-water fishing tactics are identical for both Plum Gut and the Race.

JUMP-OFF POINTS:
WATCH HILL TO PLUM GUT

Barn Island State Launch is the the shortest run to the Watch Hill Reef Complex, Rhode Island's south shore beaches, the south side of Fishers Island, and the portion of Fishers Island bordered by Long Island Sound—technically, Fishers Island Sound.

Bayberry Island State Launch in Groton is a better shot at the middle of the north side of Fishers Island, with a short run to East Point and even shorter trip to the Race Point.

Dock Road State Launch and the Niantic River State Launch are both very conveniently located for the shortest run from Connecticut to the Race and Sluiceway, the middle portion of mouth of the Sound.

The best angle to the western part of the mouth of Long Island Sound, Plum Gut, Plum Island, and the Sluiceway is from the Great Island State Launch, Lyme, Four Mile River State Launch, Old Lyme, and the Connecticut River State Launch, Old Saybrook. The best launch for larger boats is the Saybrook Launch site under I-95. Great Island is second best, but gets shallow at low tide. Four Mile River Launch is a much more difficult approach for boats capable of crossing the Sound and is probably better suited for local small-boat traffic.

14

Gardners Island, Peconic Bay, and Montauk Point

These three major fishing destinations lie across Long Island Sound, a fairly long run for anglers fishing out of Connecticut marinas or launch sites. Still, because the fishing is so good in these areas—often by starting earlier and staying later—many Connecticut boaters make the run.

Despite the fact that Montauk Point produced the IGFA's 50-pound-test record striped bass—the second biggest in sportfishing history, a monster 76-pounder to Bob Rocchetta, back in July 1981—striper fishing is good enough in the reefs and holes between Plum Gut and Watch Hill that the vast majority of Connecticut bass and bluefish enthusiasts don't go much past these productive waters to fish. It's the fluke, weakfish, and false albacore that attract the majority of anglers making the trek from the Nutmeg State.

The shallow waters and embayments along the North Shore of Long Island warm up faster and to a greater degree than the deeper, cooler waters of either the Atlantic Ocean or Long Island Sound. This means that in spring, when fish first begin migrating through the region, they are drawn like a magnet to the warm, food-rich habitats of places such as Peconic

Bay. As the waters are drawn out of this heat sink by ebbing tides and pulled to sea, they have an influence on adjacent areas. This phenomenon tends to draw striped bass then, later on, fluke, weakfish, and other warm-water-loving species into Peconic Bay when they first reach the Sound in spring.

Montauk Point is the corner all fish have to pass by when entering or leaving Long Island Sound, and Gardners Island, sitting midway between Montauk Point and Plum Gut, is a natural staging area for fish, primarily fluke, as they enter and leave the Sound each year.

During the spring, Connecticut anglers who are catching local stripers or early migrants from the Hudson River hear about the great fluke fishing off Montauk Point and in Peconic Bay. Reports of weakfish catches also filter across the Sound into local tackle shops, mobilizing anglers who are anxious to get a jump on the summer fishing season. Early on Peconic Bay is a great fishing destination, holding fluke, weakfish, striped bass, and early-run blues.

Montauk Point is a prime fluke-fishing destination early, throughout the season, and late. Due to its proximity to the fluke wintering grounds to the south and off the continental shelf, many fish move into this area early, with some filtering into and across the Sound into Connecticut waters. The majority, however, seem to hang in the tide-swept waters around Montauk Point, creating the best fluke fishery in the region as a result.

Many Connecticut-based fluke anglers who make the run across the sound stop by at Gardners Island and the nearby Ruins (an old navy fort that was used for target practice during World War II). Fluke moving into the Sound in spring then back to the ocean in fall tend to stage and therefore concentrate in the shoals around Gardners Island, creating some excellent fishing at these times as well as in between. Typically anglers will take a few drifts off Gardners; if these don't produce to their expectations, they push across the last stretch of water to Montauk Point.

In late summer and fall fluke fishermen drifting the rips and beaches on either side of Montauk Point should keep handy a spinning rod that is rigged out with a Slug-Go, Salt Shaker, Needle Eel, or other small, narrow-profile silvery plug in case a school of bonito or false albies rips past.

In fact, in fall—even during years when there are only a few scattered schools of small tuna cruising through Connecticut waters—whatever fish are in the area seem to concentrate around Montauk Point before heading back out to the open ocean where they originated. Many light-tackle and fly-rod charter boats from both New York and Connecticut waters hang out at Montauk Point, waiting for the daily surface blitzes of false albacore and bonito. Often bluefish and stripers are mixed into the fray, making for an interesting day of fishing.

Once while fluke fishing in early August, waiting for the false albacore to arrive, they started blitzing on the surface all around the area we were fishing. The fluke fishing had been poor because of a drift that pitted wind against the tide, so we quickly switched over to chasing the albies.

We readily took albacore on chrome-colored 5-inch Mambo Minnows and white 4-inch Twister Tails on jigheads that were either cast into or trolled through the surface-feeding tuna. Unlike many outings that target these fish, they were hitting with reckless abandon. Everyone on board hooked up between 10 and 20 times that afternoon.

When the falsies were ripping around the boat, we tried live-lining the big mummichogs we had brought with us for fluke baits. Fished on a size 1 Texposer hook and allowed to swim with no additional weight or just a small split shot, all the remaining mummies were chomped by the tuna, adding tremendously to our exceptional hookup rate that day.

Though we've talked about it, we have not targeted false albacore or bonito with live hook baits such as mummichogs, silversides, or snapper blues. It certainly made for some fast and furious action and would probably be equally successful under most situations, provided the baits could be dropped into the schools of tuna as they passed by. In addition to taking the tuna, these baits will draw strikes from feeding bluefish and striped bass. During the same trip when we experimented with free-lining mummichogs, one of the crew hooked and landed a 36-inch striper with a larger bait.

Another excellent method of taking schooled-up albacore is to net a pail or two of silversides and/or peanut bunker. Go to an area where the tuna are holding and begin chumming with the dead baits. Then drop fresh or live baits back into the slick on free lines, with small peg sinkers or off bobbers. Each year, progressively more anglers who are targeting these hard-to-hook fish are experimenting successfully with these standard offshore tuna-fishing methods, and landing more false albacore and bonito on the inshore grounds as a result.

PART TWO
RHODE ISLAND

15

The South Shore Beaches to Point Judith

R hode Island is essentially a huge sand dune that has been
sculpted by the Atlantic Ocean and inflowing rivers. The
result is a predominantly sandy shoreline punctuated by a
series of salt ponds leading up to Narragansett Bay, the large
indentation that defines Rhode Island's distinctive shoreline.
Though quite shallow and sandy, numerous inflowing rivers
with rock outcrops and islands across their mouths give character to this complex estuary, the largest in the region.
Approximately 10 miles off the coast lies Block Island. Its sand
beaches, distinctive bluffs, and rocky shores, are located about
halfway between Montauk Point and Martha's Vineyard, are
smack-dab in the middle of the striped bass migration route
from the south, creating one of the region's supreme striper
destinations. The combination of this state's unique and complex shoreline, numerous surf-fishing beaches, and gem of an
island off the coast makes this tiny state a giant among striped
bass enthusiasts.

From Watch Hill to Point Judith, Rhode Island's south
shore provides surf fishermen with miles of fairly accessible
beach. This stretch of nearly continuous sandy beaches is
punctuated with occasional rocky areas and four major salt

ponds, each connected to the ocean by a hard-flowing, fish-attracting breachway. Working from south to north along the coast, the first of the four ponds is Winnepaug Salt Pond, which empties into the ocean through Weekapaug Breachway. Next door is Quonochontaug Salt Pond and Breachway, often referred to by anglers as "Quonny Pond." The largest and most accessible is Ninigret Salt Pond, which dumps into the ocean through the famous and nasty Charleston Breachway. Nearly equal in size and home to Rhode Island's commercial fishing fleet and processing plants, because of its deeper and cooler harbor, is the Point Judith Salt Pond. This area is a favorite among both surf and boat fishermen, with its concrete launch ramp, long breakwall, bridges and docks inside the harbor where sportfishermen can fish but, most importantly, can catch fish of all species.

Each salt pond has a classic barrier beach separating it from the Atlantic. Quonny Breachway, Charleston Breachway, and Point Judith Salt Pond all have good state boat launch sites from which anglers can depart. Weekapaug does not have a state launch ramp, so must either be fished from shore or approached from the sea.

Each breachway usually has its own complement of bass, blues, fluke, occasional weakfish, and in season bonito and/or false albacore moving in and out from the ocean to feed on a daily basis. Fish moving up and down the beaches with the tides will stop to chow down around strong currents and rips that set up as the waters drain out of these salt ponds with the dropping tide.

Spread out as they are along about 13 miles of coastline, tidal changes will take place at a slightly different time in each of the four salt ponds, with about half an hour's difference between Point Judith and Weekapaug. For this reason it's wise to shop around to find the pond that seems to be producing the most fish; also, try to be there when the tide is high and changing to the ebb. High tide is when you should fish the channels and inside the salt ponds. Outgoing water is the best time to fish the breachways and ocean side of the breachways at all the salt ponds, because it drags fish-attracting bait out to the ocean each time they flush. When tide changes take place at dawn, at dusk, or throughout the night, that's when the surf casters have their greatest success on big striped bass. Blues, fluke, black-fish, porgies, and the tuna are more diurnal in their nature, though sunset and sunrise are always the best times to fish for these species, again as the tide is ebbing. The salt ponds also provide some fishing for hickory shad for sport or to use as big-bass bait throughout most of late spring and summer.

Hard-core surf casters will often fish Point Judith Pond or Charleston Breachway on the ebb tide. As it hits dead slack low, when the action usually stops with the movement of water, they scurry down the coast to Quonochontaug Breachway or Weekapaug Breachway to catch the last of the moving water down there for perhaps 20 to 30 minutes if they time things properly. If the fish are there and active, this tactic could add another fish or two to a day's, or night's, catch.

Jared Sampson and Rick Falvey hold four of the dozen fluke we caught this day off Misquamicut Beach. Ten-pounders have been caught here as fluke numbers grow and the population gets a chance to mature.

The salt ponds, due to their shallow nature, warm up and cool down much more rapidly than the deeper waters of the open ocean. They quickly heat up 10, 15, even 20 degrees warmer than the nearby Atlantic every spring. The result is a warm-water outflow spilling out into the Atlantic in a comparative trickle that often draws striped bass up inside, where they feed actively during the cool-water times of midspring. The shallow waters of all the salt ponds all hold a plethora of foods, including silversides, mummichogs, crabs, eels, and worms of many different species. It turns into an all-you-can-eat smorgasbord restaurant for local striped bass and bluefish that make feeding forays up inside the salt ponds with the tides. Other species such as bluefish and small tuna tend to hang around the mouths of the breachways, where they concentrate and provide anglers with some of the better fishing opportunities each season. Fluke will slide inside to feed, but also are more concentrated off the mouths during an ebbing tide. Winter flounder—or whatever is left of the winter flounder population—enter the salt ponds in fall. They spend the winter then spawn sometime after ice-out before being driven back to the cool waters of the Atlantic as water temperatures rise much over 50 or 55 degrees in spring.

One of the highlights of every striped bass season for many anglers is what is erroneously called the "cinder worm hatch." It is actually an incredible spawning event that takes place all up and down the coast when water temperatures hit the proper level. Fishing the "worm spawn" is my favorite way of catching striped bass during the course of every season.

It takes place among one of the many of species of nereid worms—close relatives to *Nereis virens*, the common clam or sandworms that fishermen buy for bait. The small worms that come out to play in Connecticut and Rhode Island waters sometime in May are (in my best estimation) *Nereis succinea*, or yellow-jawed clam worms. Every spring or early summer they swim out of their muddy burrows into the water column, by the tens or hundreds of thousands, where they disperse their genetic material in order to create a new generation and build another biological bridge through time. These 2- to 5-inch-long worms spawn in huge masses that help ensure successful mixing of their eggs and sperm, because they are broadcast spawners. They usually begin their spawning activities at a time of year when striped bass are moving by the salt ponds in their northward migration. It appears that they either smell the worms or follow the stream of prey that has to be carried out into the ocean with each evening ebb tide, then pile up inside the salt ponds or river mouths where these events are taking place.

Worm spawns are not unique to Rhode Island's salt ponds. Some form of spawning event takes place throughout the world's marine waters every year. In New England a couple of species of worms do so in large enough numbers to be noticed by both fish and fishermen. The intensity and longevity of these worm spawns vary from area to area, ranging from a night or two in some places—so they are easily missed or overlooked by local fishermen—to weeks in others. The most popular worm spawn fishing areas have worm activity that can be protracted over a period of weeks, attracting the attention of many anglers who have picked up on this unique, often productive, and extremely exciting fishing event. Whether it's long or short in duration, the fish and local wildlife, including terns, gulls, and even swans, never miss it.

I have read that the full moon, tides, and other celestial events are the key to predicting these worm spawn events. Certainly tides can make a difference in how easy or tough the fishing is, but the worms do their thing—according to my observations for over more than a decade—correlated most closely to water temperature. Other factors are secondary, at least as far as the yellow-jawed clam worms are concerned.

I've talked to fishermen from the Mill and Housatonic Rivers in western Connecticut, anglers who fish Great Bay, New

My wife Karen battles a 28-inch striper in the calm waters of Ninigret (Charleston) Salt Pond during the spring worm spawn, when bass by the thousands move into salt ponds to feed on small yellow-jawed clam worms, tiny cousins of sandworms. With shallow water and casts to breaking fish, this is the most fun way to take bass.

Hampshire, and those from rivers in southern Maine, and all have seen, fished in, or at least heard about worm spawn events. Exactly which species are involved is up for debate. Some I know to be *Nereis virens*, the common clam worm, or bait worm. *N. succinea* is much smaller—some too small to fit on a hook—but this is the species that appears to be responsible for a good portion of the worm spawn activity in eastern Connecticut and southern Rhode Island that I have observed and participated in.

Worm spawning activity takes place in literally every estuary and tide pond throughout the region in spring. Most occur sometime in the month of May, depending on weather conditions. The spawns farther north are later in the year due to the differences in warming speeds of local waters.

In the places I have monitored and fished actively the key is waters warming to 62 to 65 degrees, with this narrow temperature range being the apparent triggering temperature for worm spawning activities. Even though some years during May, water temps in the ocean are still in the 40s, the salt ponds and shoal areas of coastal estuaries where these events take place can easily be 65 or higher by this time. I've caught striped bass that were slurping worms down as early as the first or (at the latest) second week of May most years in Ninigret Salt Pond.

The key to finding a worm spawn near you is monitoring the temperatures in the tidal flat areas and large coves of local rivers, salt ponds, and other protected waters, in order to determine when they will reach the mid-60s. Spring cold snaps or heavy, chilling rains will end the progress like an "off" switch—but eventually the sun wins out, and spawning temperatures are achieved. Areas with prime worm habitat—that is, with extensive shallow, eelgrass flats—will produce huge worm spawns, while areas with harder bottoms, strong tides, and cooler temps may not be worth fishing.

The Mystic River, for example, is a typical river channel with shallow flats and a deep channel running like a gash up from Long Island Sound to the town of Mystic. Due to its direct link to the cooler waters of Long Island Sound and fairly high flushing rate, the waters of its shallows are constantly chilled back down with each flood tide, despite the fact that they may warm well into the 60s during a hot, still day when the sun is burning bright.

The worm spawn here normally takes place within three to five days of May 22, and is of short duration. One year I caught it right on the button. A few worms had been showing in the evenings for nearly a week. On Friday evening I went fishing to check out the reports. At dusk the worms came out, but were dispersed and somewhat sparse. The few feeding striped bass that were around seemed to slurp down every worm that moved up into the water column. Fishing was great; I caught 25 stripers ranging from 14 to 30 inches and saw larger fish swim by the boat in a little over an hour. Nearly every time I cast a

4½-inch-long Slug-Go to a visible surface swirl from a worm-feeding bass, it seemed to grab the lure.

On Sunday, two days later, I returned with a friend. There were at least 10 times more worms—so many they looked like raindrops on the water's surface—creating a huge dilution factor. Despite the fact that there were many more visible stripers feeding on them, our catch rate was frustratingly low. We only caught about six stripers between the two of us, and they were all small. Two days after that the worm activity was all over and the bass were in a large school in the east channel for a few days.

On the other hand, Charleston, Rhode Island's, Ninigret Salt Pond (often called Charleston Salt Pond) is a huge amorphous-shaped body of water with long shallow arms—it looks like an amoeba on a map—and a small but violent drain into the ocean through the Charleston Breachway. The flushing rate here is slower than in, say, Mystic or Point Judith Salt Pond, which both feature a relatively open drain into the ocean. For this reason the heat up inside the pond is retained more effectively in its shallow arms, driving various places up into the comfort zone for worm spawning over a longer period of time. Ninigret Salt Pond produces worms from the first week in May through early to mid-June (in oddball years when temps are cool and variable during spring). As a result, it provides the best opportunity to experience worm spawn fishing in the region.

The nebulous shape of Ninigret means that various areas heat and cool unevenly, so the worms are not necessarily all coming out of the mud throughout the pond at the same time. Rather, they seem to peak in one area one night, another place the next, and so forth, with an overall peak period when some worms can be seen literally anywhere in the pond taking place sometime in mid- to late May.

Anglers without boats can take the Ninigret State Park exit off Route 1 and walk out to the various places in the park, which borders the pond on its western edge. Some anglers launch kayaks from various drop points to search for the best, most active places within the pond.

The best way to fish the worm spawn here is definitely from a small boat. The mobility will enable you to travel easily to the various coves and inlets within the pond and locate areas where the worms are coming off on any given night. Larger boats can be launched from the state facility at the Charleston Breachway itself and run up inside. Get there by following the signs for the breachway off Route 1, then signs to the launch— a right turn off the road where it ends at the oceanfront.

A small, gravel town launch with limited parking provides access to the pond from its eastern side, off Town Dock Road, the second exit heading east past the Ninigret State Park exit off Route 1. Ocean House Marina has a private launch site, again with limited parking, that can be used for a typical launch fee. Right at the end of Town Dock Road is the "town dock," a small cartop launch that many anglers use to drop off kayaks and cartop boats free of charge. The problem is the limited parking along the road.

Of the many different and varied striped bass fisheries that develop each season, the spring worm spawn is one that every light-tackle or fly fisherman should experience. It has all the elements that make for exciting angling.

First and foremost, it's sight fishing, something that's not usually possible when marine fishing here in New England. Striped bass are abundant, sometimes to the point of being distracting, and therefore easily spotted as they leave telltale swirls when they are slurping worms on, or just beneath, the surface. The worm spawn takes place in relatively protected, shallow waters, so angling can be done from shore in some cases, but also in relative safety from a small boat, kayak, or canoe. The shallow water often makes for longer runs and quality fights. The final element is the fact that the only way to catch these fish is with a fly rod or light spinning tackle that can cast a very light, soft plastic lure.

Fly fishers have developed a number of fly patterns to "match the hatch"; these perform very well when the worms come out to play. There's no need to become anal over it, though: Any brown or light-colored pipe-cleaner-type fly will take bass. It's the presentation and action that catch the fish, rather than the pattern. I have done well using a 2-inch-plus, root-beer-colored Woolly Bugger pattern.

The secret to taking worm-feeding striped bass with regularity is paying attention. When spawning worms and feeding stripers have been located, scan the surface for a swirl within casting range and immediately fire off a cast. Bass will often run right under the surface, planning up to the top to take the worms they encounter.

From above the water this looks like a swirl with a wake leading away to another swirl. When a bass is hot and in a worm-feeding frenzy, it may make two, three, even four or five swirls in a straight line, circle, or other oddball shape, each one 5 to 10 feet from the last. This is the easiest fish to catch. Simply land a cast an appropriate distance ahead of the feeding striper, let it sink a foot or so, twitch it up to the top so that it dimples like the real worms, and hold on.

The hands-down best, most productive lure for taking worm-feeding striped bass is a 3½-inch Slug-Go. Colors are debatable. We have done well over the years by using Texas Chili and Arkansas Shiner colors when the worms are sparse and stripers numerous, or early in the evening when the worms first appear on top and the swirling begins. When worms are very abundant however—or near dusk, when visibility is reduced—use a more visible Slug-Go such as white or bubblegum pink to improve hookup percentage.

Three-inch-long Whip Stiks, 4-inch Berkley Power Sand Worms, Bass Assassins, drop shot worms, or any small plastic worm in the 3- to 4-inch range will work, but the Slug-Go is by far the king when it comes to fooling stripers during the worm spawn.

Rig whatever soft plastic is available with a 1/0 or 2/0 wide-gap hook. I prefer a 1/0 Texposer that is hooked through the Slug-Go just under the tip of its nose, with the hook totally exposed and poking out of the belly. If weeds and snagging become problems, as they can during low tide, fish the lure weedless style by slipping the hook shallow under the nose, pushing it out the bottom, reversing its direction, and sticking it out the back of the lure. This is called Texas rigging by freshwater bass fishermen, who have been weedless rigging this way for generations.

The trick is casting these small, light, but not-so-aerodynamic lures. The Whip Stik is the best of the lot to cast into a headwind. From a boat it's usually possible to maneuver so that you can use the wind to help carry these light lures to the fish.

Tackle for this style of fishing must be light yet powerful. Ideally, cast with a 7- to 7½-foot, medium-action spinning rod; for added casting distance, with a reel that balances nicely with the rod. The key is the line. Berkley Fireline in 6- or 8-pound test is the most practical for larger bass when they burrow down into the eelgrass, though 4-pound-test Fireline will cast anything a long distance with a 7-foot lever. The 4-pound test is more likely to break under stress of a fish and weeds, while the 6- and 8-pound can handle most situations with no problems because they cut through the weeds like a Weed Whacker. I have caught stripers up to 25 or 30 pounds with this outfit rigged out with 6-pound-test Fireline. Monofilament of the same caliber would not have done the job in the pre-Fireline era of fishing. Other superbraids, though strong enough, are also thicker or rougher, thus creating more friction. They simply do not cast as well as slick black Fireline, which we tie directly to the hook using a double improved clinch knot, uniknot or Trilene knot, with no leader of any sort.

This light versatile, great casting rig not only makes every bass fun to catch—even the small ones—but it also allows for fast, accurate casting. Once when I was fishing between two of my fly-rodding buddies, the ability to open the bail and immediately fire a cast to a surface-feeding, worm-slurping striped bass allowed me to outfish both of them combined by a factor of two or three to one during the worm spawn. They simply could not get their casts to the fish quickly enough; even when they did, false casts that slapped the line on top of the fish frequently scared them away.

One of these two friends, for some noble reason that I can't fathom, totally gave up spin fishing in favor of "the long rod with the short cast." I think that stupid movie *A River Runs Through It* ruined his perspective somehow.

Now on every worm spawn trip with him, as he goes through his rod-rigging ritual for about 15 minutes before he gets started, I make a standard comment that makes him wince every time. Just as he unsheathes his rod from the case I say: "I see you'd still rather cast than catch fish."

We have a good laugh, me harder than him, because on one trip he had to borrow a spare spinning rod rigged with a Slug-Go to get deskunked. He caught a striper within two casts, then went back to "casting." It was windy, and the fish were picky that day. So ribbing him about it is unfair, but then again, life's not always fair. It did provide me with the ultimate weapon in the friendly banter that always takes place when friends go fishing.

Look for shorter but equally excellent worm spawn fishing in Point Judith Salt Pond, Quonny Salt Pond, Little Narragansett Bay (on the Connecticut border), Narragansett Bay, Green River, and other tidal areas in this state well endowed with tidal estuaries.

Overall, the salt ponds are a great asset to fishermen who come to Rhode Island for the great fishing it provides. Especially in spring and fall, when large numbers of fish concentrate inside and off their breachways, the salt ponds provide surf casters and boat fishermen alike with an easy-to-locate, easily accessible spot that almost always hold some fish. The best action takes place from dusk through dawn, but during spring and fall both predators and prey will be hanging around every time the water is flowing out of these areas. Boat fishermen naturally have the ability to run the beaches and work the breachways from the outside casting in—a great advantage when it comes to catching striped bass and other popular gamefish species.

Rhode Island has some of the best striper fishing on the planet. Back in the 1960s, Charleston Breachway produced 50- and 60-pound striped bass that temporarily claimed both men's and women's line-class world records. When roaming the beaches for stripers, look for birds, reefs, and rocks. The original scientific name for striped bass (now called *Morrone saxatilis*, demonstrating its phylogenetic relationship to white perch) was *Roccus saxatilis*—literally "rock of the rocks." This statement is never more true than where a seascape is primarily sand, as along much of the Rhode Island coast. Anyplace there are rock piles, ledges, jetties, or breachways, there will be striped bass.

Stripers chasing bait along the open sand beaches will tend to concentrate along drop-offs, in deeper holes, or in trenches that are dug out by regular tidal action or inflowing breachways.

Besides providing excellent fishing for striped bass and bluefish, the south shore beaches often have small tuna running up and down with the tides; like stripers and blues, they stop occasionally to feed in front of a breachway or around the rips over the top of a reef. The best places, even more productive than the breachways to seek these fish are the breakwalls off Point Judith, at the north end of this stretch of predominantly sand beaches, or at the end of the line, over the reefs at Watch Hill.

As everywhere else, winter flounder fishing has dropped nearly off the charts. There are, however, still a small number of winter flounder caught in Weekapaug and Quonny Salt Ponds, and a few more than that in the Point Judith Pond, which is cooler and has a much greater flushing rate than the somewhat warmer salt ponds to the south. At best, winter flounder fishing in these locations is only a faint shadow of what it was before overfishing took its toll.

In Rhode Island winter flounder fisheries were particularly hard hit, because in this state, where commercial interests held biologists and management at bay, until the populations crashed back in the early 1980s small trawlers were allowed to harvest these fish from the salt ponds, where they spent the winter and spawned. A classic example of management being bullied by powerful, politically connected commercial concerns.

Fluke fishing is always excellent along the entire Rhode Island coast, and the south shore beaches always shine as bright spots. Due to the migration pathways that fluke follow as they move northward and inshore in spring, they tend to hit the coastline north of Long Island at or very near Point Judith and the mouth of Narragansett Bay. Most likely, the warm water flowing out of the bay and this large salt pond is the primary attractant for these warm-loving fish.

In most years the legions of Rhode Island commercial rod-and-reel anglers—who always get in a month of fishing before everyone else—begin catching fluke from the drifts outside and south of Point Judith around the first week of May. Two weeks to a month before anyone fishing in eastern Long Island Sound can go out fluke fishing with any confidence of success, anglers can fish anywhere from the opening of the West Wall at Galilee to Greenhill or even Misquamicut and catch fluke. The fish seem to show earliest and in abundance between Point Judith and Nebraska Shoal; within a few days to a week, they begin spreading southward toward Long Island Sound.

The Sound has some fluke filtering in through Plum Gut and the Race, fed by fish pushing around the corner at Montauk Point. In the easternmost gap across the Sound, between Fishers Island and the mainland, some fluke always seem to start at the north end of the south shore of Rhode Island and work their way into the Sound from there.

With the regulations in all southern New England states changing practically from season to season, a discussion of strategies working with these regulations isn't appropriate. Still, it is fair to note that increases in minimum fluke lengths during the 2001 and 2002 seasons—which will probably remain pretty much as they are for a while into the future—have made taking limits of fish much more challenging across the board. So if you're seeking fluke out of Barn Island or the south shore of Rhode Island and able to fish the waters of all three states in a single trip, you need to be aware of the differences in regulations.

Because the regulations are possession limits that are applicable to whatever state you happen to be fishing in at the time, where the fish were caught doesn't matter. When you change fishing locales, then, it's wise to go by the lowest common denominator—in other words, stick to the most restrictive regulations among the states you may be fishing in order to be legal in all.

Even though fluke are bottomfish that prefer relatively clean, clear stretches of sand or small-gravel bottom, like any predator they seek cover to aid them in ambushing their prey. Because fluke are the ultimate camouflaged predator, attacking their prey like a piece of the bottom coming up unseen from below or behind, they will hide near rocks, ledges, or drop-offs to gain an advantage. Fluke often hold just over the edges or lips of drop-offs or channel edges to ambush hapless prey items that may be swept by the tides, or swim over the edge of the drop-off.

For this reason, when you're choosing a setup for fluke—which will depend on the prevailing tide and winds—try to find a drift that runs either along the edge of or over the lip of a drop-off. The drop-off needn't be a large one. I have had good success at drop-offs from 30 to as little as 32 or 34 feet, nestled between two 26-foot-high underwater plateaus. The fluke seem to run across the high spots and concentrate within 20 yards of the edge, where it drops from 26 to 30 feet.

The southern Rhode Island coastline is fairly nondescript, with anglers often using visible, man-made landmarks such as various homes to determine where to fish. "The Pink House" between Watch Hill and Misquamicut Beach is a famous fluke-fishing destination, for example. You'll also find the Blue House, the Andrea Hotel, the Merry-Go-Round, and other landmarks to go by along the south shore beaches. Landmarks are not as important as what lies below the surface when it comes to catching fluke, anywhere.

The best way to find a good fluke drift along the south shore beaches is to get a chart and look at the contour lines, then seek them out with the depth finder. Locate places where there are underwater points that lead out into deeper water a half a mile or so off the beach. Look for slightly deeper troughs—which often change with major storms—that lead out from the beach into deeper water. Fish the edge of the major drop-off, where waters change from 20 to 30 feet out to 50 or 60 feet. The fluke often hold along this slope or just along the transition zone at the bottom or top of this structure.

Holes blown out of the bottom by an inflowing breachway, and humps created by the material blown out of those holes such as Nebraska Shoal, are all excellent fluke-fishing areas.

The key to successful fluke fishing is determining the relationship of wind and tide in the area you plan to fish. It is imperative that wind and tide be running together or, at worst, that the wind be blowing across the prevailing tides. The flood tide tends to flow south along the south shore beaches as it fills Fishers Island Sound, and north when it drains. Given that prevailing winds during the summer months are out of the south, southwest, or west, the flood tide can often be unproductive, especially when wind and tide are directly against each other.

For this reason, if you're planning a fluke-fishing trip to the south shore (or anywhere else), consult the Weather Channel (which offers more accurate wind speed and direction predictions than local weather stations on TV) and choose destinations based on how winds and tides will be behaving. Again, it's best to drift at a fast pace with wind and tide together, which can be controlled by a drift sock. If wind and tide are against each other—with lines running under the boat and movement minimal—forget it. Baits will move so slowly that undesirable species such as skate or crabs will have a chance to chew on and ruin expensive baits. Only a change of tide or wind direction will solve this problem.

When I know the winds won't be favorable, I simply don't tempt fate by fishing in what I know to be horrible conditions. I either stay home, aim for a different species such as striped bass, or find a protected place to get out of the wind.

Nebraska Shoal off Point Judith is a famous fluke-fishing destination that gives up a fair percentage of the doormats logged in at tackle shops between Charleston and Point Judith every summer. Three decades ago, before bluefin tuna were decimated by commercial overharvest, Nebraska Shoal was perhaps the best nearshore giant-tuna area outside Cape Cod's Stellwagen Bank.

I remember fishing in the U.S. Atlantic Tuna Tournament (USATT) out of Point Judith during the early 1970s. That event was won by a boat called the *Black Stallion* fishing out of Groton, Connecticut. The crew hooked an 820-pound giant bluefin tuna off Nebraska Shoal within sight of our boat and landed the fish in about 20 feet of water off one of the beaches nearby.

In those days surf fishermen occasionally observed giant tuna feeding on the menhaden, mackerel, and sometimes even the bluefish they were trying to catch just beyond the surf break anywhere from the Charleston Breachway to Narragansett Beach. Unfortunately those days are gone, though hopefully not forever. If the tuna are allowed to recover and the population is allowed to mature and grow, they will probably return to these historic fishing grounds . . . where someone like me could have a go at one in a small boat.

16
Block Island

A satellite photo of the East Coast readily shows the moraines left behind by the continental glaciers as they receded 20,000 years ago. Tracing a line along the seaward edge of Long Island and running it straight at that angle until it hits the mainland, you'll see what looks like a string of widely spaced pearls beginning with the world's striped bass mecca, Cuttyhunk Island, and ending at the Elizabeth Island chain. Block Island is on that line, roughly a third of the distance from Montauk Point to Massachusetts waters.

It isn't too much of a stretch to picture the annual north–south migration of striped bass that originates in Chesapeake Bay traveling along the coast of Long Island and streaming across, first to Block Island, then to Cuttyhunk and the Elizabeth Islands, with fish breaking off and sprinkling in along the Rhode Island, New York, and Connecticut coasts in the process.

It's debatable which of these three incredibly good striped bass grounds is the best. Taking aesthetics out of the picture— all three spots are gorgeous—the recordbook may be the most objective way to shine some light on this argument.

The all-tackle world record is the 78½-pound monster taken from Atlantic City, New Jersey, during the fall run of 1982.

The Southeast Light at Block Island overlooks one of the most famous stretches of striper water anywhere. Countless huge bass have been wrenched from the rocks below, including a 60-pound-plus monster taken by Tim Coleman during the great giant striper blitzes of the late 1970s and early 1980s.

All the current monsters, striped bass of 70 pounds or more, come from Connecticut and New York. There is a 57-pound women's world record from Block Island, along with a 56-pounder from Gay Head on Martha's Vineyard, and Bob Rochetta's 76-pounder from Montauk Point. Back in the early 1980s Block Island held two records and Cuttyhunk one, a 72-pounder. Over time Tony Stetsko caught his famous 73-pounder at Provincetown on the Cape, and Tim Coleman—the former editor of *The Fisherman* magazine's New England edition—caught a 67-pounder from the surf at Block Island. The year Coleman made his impressive catch, a number of 50-pound-plus stripers were taken from the whitewater around the Block.

Each of the "pearls" along this string of islands has produced its share of 60-pound-plus stripers, and Block Island is right up there with the best of them.

Unlike its nearby cousin, Fishers Island, Block Island is a summer tourist destination, with daily ferry runs between

Point Judith, Rhode Island and New London, Connecticut, importing droves of tourists throughout the season. Most are there to shop, enjoy the quaint scenery, and ride mopeds or butt-breaking rental bikes around the island's coastal road. Throughout the season, particularly during spring and fall, a legion of dedicated surf fishermen flock to Block Island in the hope of catching one of those monster stripers that lurk along its rocky shores. Many anglers make the run across in private boats to fish for striped bass and fluke, though some do so to target black seabass, a species that has been gaining in popularity over the past decade.

Block has long been a jumping-off point for offshore fishermen who make the long runs to the tuna, shark, and billfishing grounds between Nomans Land, offshore from Cuttyhunk, to Block Island Canyon and the famous Fishtails south of Montauk Point. It's smack-dab in the middle of everything, in other words—that's why it's such great fishing.

Access to the shore is not complete, but it's not bad compared to the Connecticut coast. You can essentially fish from any of 14 public access points around the island's coastline. Two are found on each side of the Block Island National Wildlife Refuge at the northern tip.

Running off this shark-tooth-shaped point is a shoal that continues nearly a mile out into the ocean, creating the famous North Rips. Shore-based fishermen can walk to the tip of the island and out onto this sandbar, where they can cast to striped bass, bluefish, fluke, and (in season) false albacore, bonito, and possibly a mackerel or two.

Many charter and private boats run across from Rhode Island and Connecticut to these waters throughout the season. I have had the pleasure of fishing with my good friend Captain Al Anderson of the charter boat *Prowler* on a couple of occasions, as well as other trips from private boats. Captain Al single-handedly holds just about every fish-tagging record kept by the American Littoral Society.

In spring, when the big bass collect to feed along the North Rips, all you need to do is pull up to the visible rip line and keep the boat steady by running into the current fast enough to hold in one position or anchor. Ebb tide is best, but any moving water will create fish-holding currents. If possible avoid running over the rip—especially with the engines running—because it will scatter the fish and ruin the fishing in that area.

Once you're in place, simply drop baits such as eels or chunks back into the rips, or cast lures. In the past we have caught numerous bass up to about 40 inches on light tackle by casting Fin-S fish ranging from 5½ to 10 inches. Speed jigging would also work well in this area when the fish are stacked.

There are deep holes off the tip of the North Rip—great spots to drop an eel or jig down deep with a three-way rig. As everywhere else, the bigger striped bass tend to spend most of their time in deeper waters, occasionally traveling into shoal areas to feed. For this reason, you can improve your odds of taking a jumbo fish by moving to where they are likely to be, rather than waiting for one to come to you.

A good strategy for fishing this area is to cast the rips as the sun sets or rises, and fish bait or jigs in the deep holes at the tip after dark.

Moving along the west side of the island, a great shore-fishing spot can be found at the Coast Guard station near the breakwall the mouth of Great Salt Pond, where it dumps into the Atlantic. Gamefish move through this "gateway" to the ocean with the prevailing tides. Surf fishermen will wait there after dark with lures or live eels and catch the striped bass and blues that are constantly chasing bait in and out of the salt pond.

During the 1980s, while fishing in the U.S. Atlantic Tuna Tournament—which was based at Block Island for a few years in a row—the New London Tuna Club won a record-setting three consecutive tournaments. Two of those wins came because of the live bait we caught during the event.

The Coast Guard station at Great Salt Pond, Block Island, is always a great place to fish from shore. Bass and blues usually move in and out with the tides. Sometimes bonito and false albacore move in to provide some additional challenges.

I was fishing on a boat for hire with friends; owned and operated by Captain Mario Pagano, it was aptly named the *Fish Trap*. A shrewd fisherman who specialized in giant bluefin tuna, Mario always shunned frozen baits. Contestants had to start off with the bait provided by the tournament, but it was legal to use any live baits that were captured while out on the water.

The first year fishing off the *Fish Trap*, Captain Pagano had us all go out for a leisurely breakfast so we would be the last boat to leave for the fishing grounds. This didn't make sense to me at first, but there was a method to his madness.

After breakfast we ran back to Point Judith to catch some mackerel off the West Breakwall. We then brought them back to the grounds, having invested two hours of fishing time with our bait-catching efforts. Once we were on the grounds, it took less than an hour to hook up with a tournament-winning 520-pound bluefin tuna.

The second year, after all the boats left for the offshore grounds, we got on board, ran the boat a few hundred yards from Champlain's Marina out into Great Salt Pond, took out the Scotty rigs, and quickly caught a dozen live macks for bait.

We followed the same maneuver every morning, offering various excuses—"So-and-so drank too much"; "So-and-so overslept"—to neighboring boats for our late starts.

The time we invested in catching live bait was worth it. We landed a limit of giant bluefins—five fish per week at that time—all on live mackerel. The smart thinking and bait supplied by Great Salt Pond won the tournament that year based on total pounds. The five 310-pound-plus "giant tuna" were enough to beat out another boat's 1,142-pound behemoth—the largest tuna ever caught in the 50-plus-year history of the USATT—by a few pounds.

The outflow of the salt pond has given up bluefish, striped bass, and bonito to us while we fished from the rocks on one or two fall trips to the island. From a boat, the channel it etches into the bottom for a ways offshore is a great area to drift for fluke. Down a short distance from the Coast Guard station is Charleston Beach, a small access point to a rocky shoreline that comes off the coastal road as it bends and heads toward the center of the island. Farther south, as the road heads back closer to the shore again, at the junction of Conneymus Road and West Side Road you'll find a small right-of-way path that leads to Southwest Point. This southwest corner of Block Island is a fishing hot spot from both surf and boat. A fair number of the big striped bass taken from the surf at Block Island have come from this famous stretch of rocky shoreline.

Some of the best striper fishing anywhere is found over the top of the shoal waters that extend off the southwestern corner of Block Island where its picturesque bluffs begin. The shallowest spots are rocks and boulders around Southwest Ledge that come to within 23 feet of the surface. The shoals average 30 to 40 feet running back to the island, with water depths averaging 60 to 70 feet surrounding this submerged high spot.

The fishing is nothing short of phenomenal when the bass are in. Most of the charter boats troll this area with wire line and bucktails or swimming plugs with great success. Anglers who don't like the work and lack of sensitivity involved with running wire or lead-core rigs can troll using lighter tackle, along with some of the modern deep-diving lures made by Mann or Rapala, and do nearly as well. We have had great success fishing with Mann's Stretch 25+ and 30+ deep-diving lures dragged straight off heavy spinning rigs spooled with 20- to 30-pound-test Fireline, or light musky-sized bait-casting outfits spooled with 50- to 150-pound Berkley Whiplash Line.

Small bass can be caught anywhere along the beaches, but the bigger bass taken here average anywhere from 20 pounds on up to 50 pounds or more. Every year numerous 50-pound bass are caught in this stretch of water, mostly by charter fishermen who have the trolling passes and drifts down cold.

The entire west side of the island is a great area to fish for fluke when the winds and tides are right. If possible, drift the boat in 30 to 50 feet of water—a relatively narrow contour in this area. In addition to fluke, you can expect to catch some black seabass, especially when your drifts come close to the prevalent rock structure.

One of the more picturesque vistas at Block Island is Mohegan Bluffs. Many tourists seek out this spot for the gorgeous view and photo opportunities it provides. At the end of Pilot Hill Road is a path that leads down to the water via a steep climb to the surf.

A tad farther down Southeast Light Road is the Southeast Lighthouse. This famous destination was actually moved back from the eroding bluffs recently to prevent it from tumbling into the Atlantic. Mohegan Bluffs is perhaps the most popular tourist destination on the island, with its gorgeous view of the ocean and famous wooden staircase. We dubbed this the

"Stairway to Hell" one night as we blew arteries out of our collective hearts walking back up the steps after an evening of fruitless surf casting to the Seven Sisters, a famous string of rocks leading out to sea from the base of the cliffs. The Seven Sisters is one of the places that has given up 50- and 60-pound striped bass.

This stretch of rocks at the base of Mohegan Bluffs is among the better striper-fishing stretches of shoreline on the entire coast. Tim Coleman caught his 67-pound-plus striper off this spot back in 1981, the year when so many monster bass— the end of the line, so to speak—were caught here, at Montauk Point, on the Cape, and elsewhere.

Naturally, casting into the rocks or trolling from a boat is even more productive because of the versatility it provides. The entire shoreline here is rocky, with a fairly rapid slope down to about 40 feet—ideal habitat for big striped bass.

Around the corner and heading northward along the eastern side of Block Island is Ballard's Beach, owned and operated by the famous Ballard's Inn and Marina, the mainstay for fishermen laying over in Old Harbor. Ballard's has a regionally famous shore dinner and has been a landmark on the island for more than half a century. There is ample parking and good fishing after hours and during the off season. Nearby is Old Harbor, protected by a jetty that seems to always have some striped bass and blackfish around its base and fluke in the channel.

Farther north on Corn Neck Road is Fredrick Benson Town Beach and, at its northern end, a second access off Scotch Beach Road. Fishing is not allowed when swimmers are around, but after dark and during the off season blues and bass often push bait along this stretch of water.

The shallow shelf in this area is wider, making for a better area in which to drift for fluke, though most boats fish the western edge of the island, which is closer to Connecticut and southern Rhode Island ports. Drift this shallow shelf in 20 to 50 feet for the best odds of hooking into some decent fluke, possibly a doormat of 10 pounds or more.

The last public access, with limited parking, on this side of the island is a small, sandy right-of-way at the end of Mansion Drive. Down below the bluffs is a public beach great for picnicking, swimming, fishing, and wildlife observation. Bluefish, bass, and fluke would be the primary targets here, though when the small tuna are around they occasionally push bait against the shoreline, where they come into range of surf fishermen.

Still, the best spots on the island—with their fish-attracting, sun-warmed outflows on every tide—are the entrance to New Harbor and the Great Salt Pond at the Coast Guard station, and the nearby North Rips.

17

Narragansett Bay

A round the corner from Point Judith Light lies a mile or so of beautiful classic white beaches: Scarborough and Narragansett. Both are swimming beaches fished after hours and during the off season by surf casters. They are located along a nearly straight stretch of coastline between Narragansett Bay and the south shore beaches.

There are two launch sites along these beaches. The first is off Ocean Road in Narragansett; the second is near the mouth of the Narrow River, where Route 1A crosses.

The Narrow River—actually the Pettaquamscutt—is a somewhat unusual tidal estuary draining a couple of freshwater lakes that sport excellent herring runs in spring. This, combined with a shallow brackish estuary near its mouth, makes for an excellent destination that holds and produces all varieties of fish throughout the season.

The mouth of the Narrow River near Cormorant Point is an excellent boat-fishing area for stripers, bluefish, and fluke in summer. This is one of those areas where the fish seem to arrive in early spring. Pettaquamscutt Cove is essentially another small salt pond, though not a classic one cut off from the ocean by a barrier beach. It is really a wide section in the lower river, with a slightly faster flushing rate into the ocean than the other true salt ponds to the south.

Early on—from the time striped bass first reach the region in May—anglers catch live herring from the Gilbert Stuart Homestead and live-line them in the channels and around the mouth of the Narrow River. Many folks fish successfully from and around the Middle Bridge Road bridge over the river in the saltwater section of this estuary.

The Narrow River is one of the deep-water estuaries along the coast that holds a few striped bass through the winter. You won't find the kind of developed and viable winter striper fishery that's offered by, say, the Thames River. Still, the fact that anglers catch striped bass nearly year-round indicates the presence of fish here during the off season. As in the Thames River, the abundance of food in the estuary draws striped bass into the protected, warmed waters, where they overstay their welcome and get trapped when winter temperatures blast into the area.

It's a fishy place that draws a good deal of attention from anglers in the area. In addition to the normal fare such as winter flounder, fluke, bluefish, striped bass, herring, and occasional weakfish (squeteague, in Rhode Island lingo), there are also some sea-run trout hanging around from time to time. As in many tidal estuaries throughout the region, trout drop down from lakes and streams into tidal waters, where the abundant nourishment grows them as fast as—or faster than—most hatcheries.

Look for sea-run trout action, primarily from brown trout, which seem to do better in the salt. Brookies occasionally make it in the marine environment as well, but much less frequently in southern New England waters. The best fishing for sea-run trout is during cold weather—from before the ice appears in November through and just beyond ice-out in March—with a few fish possibly lingering in the upper portions of any sea-run stream or estuary through early May, when water temperatures become uncomfortably warm.

Narragansett Bay itself is one of the better fishing destinations in the region. Conanicut (Jamestown) Island, Prudence

Island, and Aquidneck Island are the three major features across the mouth of the lower bay. There are also many smaller islands, outcrops, estuaries, and rock piles in the area that create fish-attracting-and-holding structure. The upper bay is riddled with rivers, estuaries, coves, and inlets. The combination is a unique tidal estuary that provides a wide range of fishing habitats and opportunities to catch everything on the southern New England fishing menu.

Narragansett Bay is shallow and warms up more rapidly than the ocean, thus drawing fish in from the cooler Atlantic early each spring. Winter flounder fishing remains poor here, as in most of the rest of southern New England. As the season progresses, however, striped bass enter early and provide some excellent and fast action in the shallow, warm waters from the Providence River south. The bigger bass make a showing sometime in late May or June, chasing herring and worm spawns as they occur, but for the most part they vacate the warmer waters of the upper bay as summertime temperature regimes take over. They are replaced by bluefish, which hang around in the warmer waters of the upper bay, along with some school bass during summer and early fall.

Weakfish (squeteague) are another annual visitor to Narragansett Bay. In fact, the bay has come to support one of the more fishable populations in the region as this once beleaguered species has begun to rebound. The channel along the north end of Prudence Island, and nearby Sally Rock Point at Goddard State Park, are two places that consistently produce squeteague. They're also caught sporadically throughout the bay, however, mostly by fishermen tossing small jigs or swimming plugs for school bass.

Fluke fishing is also excellent in Narragansett Bay, with the best, most consistent catches generally coming from both the west and east passages where the Jamestown and Newport bridges connect their respective islands to each other and the mainland. When the tide is dropping, the water moves at a brisk pace, excellent for fluking. The problem can be in the fact that summer winds often blow out of the south and southwest directly into the bay, funneling up through the passages. This situation could make for some difficult drifting when wind and tides are at odds. The abundance of twists, turns, and islands that may block the wind can and should be used to find the best combination of wind and tide for a given set of weather and tide conditions.

Wickford Harbor and, farther north, Greenwich Bay consistently produce catches of summer flounder, some of doormat proportions throughout the summer. As in other areas throughout the region, when the peanut bunker and other small baitfish move into Narragansett Bay, fluke will often move up inside into some very skinny water in pursuit of this abundant food source. Most anglers do not pick up on this phenomenon, but it's a good bet when juvenile bunker are swimming anywhere; whether there are bass and blues on them or not, odds are you'll find some fluke are down below. Try fishing with jigs down to a quarter ounce in weight baited with a small strip of squid and, if possible, a live mummichog. Drop this offering into some peanut bunker and it's possible to catch blues, weakfish, or stripers in this area.

Conanicut Island has three state parks, each including a different point, which allows surf fishermen to move from place to place in order to hit various tidal conditions and even find spots where the wind is at their backs rather than in their faces.

Fort Getty State Park is situated at a place called Beaverhead, on the northern tip of a peninsula on the southwest corner of Conanicut Island. This park is situated facing predominantly north and into the west passage out of Narragansett Bay. It's at the end of Fort Getty Road, a right turn off Beavertail Road leading across the hourglasslike constriction between the southwestern end of Jamestown and the main island. Fort Getty Park has both a fishing pier and a concrete launch site, which provides easy access to the west passage and its excellent fluke and striper opportunities.

At the end of Beavertail Road lies Beavertail State Park and its picturesque lighthouse. The rocks at this famous spot provide surf fishermen with some of the best whitewater in this part of the state. Every season numerous large bass are caught from the rocks by anglers casting either from the surf or from boats. Most of the big stuff is typically caught using live eels or chunk baits after dark. When possible, fishing menhaden or live hickory shad around these tide-swept waters is a great way to up your odds of catching a monster striped bass. Bluefish also frequent these waters as they move into and out of the bay with tides and changing water temperatures. Naturally, rocks like these attract tautog and scup, though most angling pressure is targeted on stripers and bluefish.

On the southeastern corner of the main portion of Jamestown Island lies Fort Wetherill State Park. Its rocky shoreline is full of character and angles to work the wind into your favor when casting from the surf. It's a good place to bring the family for a picnic near the ocean. The old fort is fun to explore, and the rocky shoreline holds some giant bass.

Fort Wetherill is reached off Route 138 to Conanicut Avenue; take Wolcott Avenue, following it to Fort Wetherill Road. There is one parking lot close to the surf and its complex, varied shoreline. This is a great but potentially dangerous place to surf fish, being out in the teeth of the wind and tides of the east passage between Jamestown and Aquidneck Islands. Boaters need to be careful, because if you lose power the prevailing winds can push you into the rocks in short order.

In Jamestown proper there's a small boat launch off East Shore Road. The town docks are also found in that area, but may not always be open to fishing due to public traffic in the area.

Just north of the Newport bridge is Potter Cove, a backwater area somewhat off the main flow of the East Passage and in lee of the rocky whitewater fishing sites of southern Conanicut Island. This is one of those hit-or-miss places worth trying out on a flood tide, especially during low-light periods. Bait may move or be chased into the cove, drawing bass, blues, and (in summer and fall) false albacore or bonito in to feed.

Across the Newport bridge lies Aquidneck Island, a long island stretching almost to East Providence along the eastern side of Narragansett Bay. It's cut off from the mainland by the Sakonnet River to the east and the East Passage out of the bay to the west. A good portion of the western edge of the island is owned by the U.S. Navy, and out of bounds. Still, there are some top-notch fishing spots along the southern tip of the island where it meets the Atlantic.

Fort Adams State Park lies almost directly across the East Passage from Fort Wetherill State Park. The fort is most easily reached by taking Thames Street off Route 138 in Newport; travel straight onto Carroll Avenue, make a right onto Harrison Avenue, then turn right again onto Fort Adams Road. Like its neighbor, this is a great family destination, with picnic areas and the fort itself to explore. In addition to its rugged, rocky shoreline, Fort Adams provides anglers with a concrete launch ramp; it's a great jumping-off point to the reefs and rocky shores in the lower portion of Narragansett Bay. The fort was built in the early to mid-1800s and was taken over by the state of Rhode Island in 1965. It's now used as the location for the Newport Jazz Festival each summer.

The western edge of this park is more rugged and tide-swept, providing excellent fishing for striped bass, bluefish, occasional weakfish, and tautog (blackfish). The drop-off here is steep, so the fish are often tucked in close to shore; surf casters should make casts parallel to shore in order to tempt stripers that may be literally under their feet.

Around the corner in the more protected Newport Harbor you may find good fishing for snapper bluefish in season, hickory shad when they are around, and both winter and summer flounder, during the appropriate seasons. Winter flounder fishing here, like everywhere else, is hit or miss—mostly miss.

Across Newport Harbor from the fort is Goat Island, with all its marinas and boating facilities. The causeway leading to the island provides an excellent fishing spot for snapper bluefish, tinker mackerel, hickory shad, and fluke, along with bluefish, bass, and small tuna when they chase bait this far into the harbor. It's a protected, relatively safe spot. The biggest problem can be finding a good place to park, so fish during off hours and seasons. It's located in downtown Newport: Simply travel along the waterfront on Washington Street, then take a right onto Goat Island Causeway. Parking is on the east side of the causeway, before you make the turn to cross the bridge. There is a small boat-launch site located off Washington Street as well, but I wouldn't want to think about parking even a small trailer there during the tourist season.

Late-summer and fall blitzes of bluefish and striped bass frequently create scenes of carnage like this as fish push bait to the top and birds ambush them from above.

Brenton Point is one of those supergreat, rugged, sometimes hard-to-fish whitewater spots that offer classic New England surf-fishing habitat. During spring and fall when bass are on the move, this is a local hot spot that produces many of the big fish that make their way into various fishing reports and magazine articles. It's a short drive from Fort Adams—simply follow Harrison Avenue to Ridge Road. Parking is on the left as the road winds around the point. As with many coastal state parks, you'll want to fish this place early or late in the day; otherwise it's like the Stop & Shop deli—take a ticket. Most serious striper fishermen go to places like this during the spring and fall runs or after dark in summer.

This park is another great picnic spot, though it lacks a fort to explore. Brenton Point is a broad, rugged tide- and windswept point with a rock jetty off its western corner. Tautog can be caught around its rocks in season, but this is a prime striped bass destination that also sees bluefish and small tuna ripping by during the warm months. It's a famous big-bass spot that produced a 50-pounder a month before this book was completed. The angler was fishing in to the shore from a boat with a needlefish plug.

Off the coast lies Brenton Reef, one of the best big-striper reefs of all the offshore reefs discussed in these pages. Lying parallel to the prevailing currents, Brenton Reef is a classic place to catch big bulls and cows. It offers deep water close to a rocky shoreline, in Brenton Point and nearby Conanicut Island. It's also swept by strong tides that run along the reef parallel to the angle of the shore, which carry an endless supply of food to the waiting striped bass.

My earliest recollection of the kind of fishing this place can produce was decades ago, before the striped bass disappeared. The father of a close friend's wife was a longtime commercial rod-and-reel fisherman. Like many members of his generation, he worked a full-time job during the winter and fished hard evenings or weekends. This guy was such a successful fisherman over in Rhode Island—which has always catered to anyone wishing to make a buck by fishing—that he would quit his day job each spring when the striped bass showed up and do nothing but rape the fish with every tide. He made more money catching bass than punching in at his nine-to-five job, though the fishing probably required more overall effort and stamina.

One year we stopped by at the place he camped for the summer, located on the southern tip of Jamestown Island, for a Fourth of July picnic. When we arrived, his wife was ticked, because he and a couple of his cronies hadn't come in from their usual full night of fishing. She was afraid the boat had broken down, and he hadn't started the charcoal for the burgers yet.

He was tardy, as it turned out, because the fishing had been so good that their greed wouldn't allow them to stop. Uncharacteristically, the big bass continued to take live eels long after the sun rose. They stopped only after they ran out of bait.

They pulled into the dock just before noon. I was both appalled and impressed by their catch. As they pulled in from the sea, we could see that the boat was riding slow and low in the water. The deck of the 24-foot craft was completely covered with 20- to near-50-pound stripers. The only place it was possible to see the flooring was where the three men stood. A sad example of human greed and how good striped bass fishing can be when the fish are stacked up at a classic fishing area such as Brenton Reef.

The reef also produces its share of bluefish—which, when the bass began to decline in the late 1970s, drove these men out of the commercial sale business. They got tired of feeding expensive eels to the choppers, which made them into "cigar butts" (as we used to call an eel that had been bluefish bit).

Another time this same commercial rod-and-reel fisherman caught a small bluefish one evening on one of his last eels. The fish was what we would call a harbor blue of about 2 pounds. Given that he and his crew often live-lined bunker of about this size, he stuck a hook into the small blue and tossed it back into the inky depths of what was a dark, foggy evening. A fish picked it up that he immediately knew was much heavier and stronger than any striper he'd ever caught. After about 10 minutes he realized that it was not a big bluefish or striper, because his pool-cue rod with its 50-pound-test line and wire leader would have wiped about anything he had ever hooked in less time.

After about 30 or 40 minutes, he was thinking that maybe he was into a record-class striper—60, 70, maybe even 80 pounds! When his big fish swirled near the surface, then, he flipped on a light to take a look. Yes, a light will often make a fish run and fight even longer and scatter other bass that may be nearby; curiosity simply got the better of him.

What he saw was scary. It was not a striper, but a shark, a big barrel-chested shark, that he said was a gray-brown color and perhaps 6 or 7 feet in length. He woke the guy he was fishing with and asked him to gaff his catch. He wanted to get it back to shore both to show off, and to get it out of the waters his family often swam in just a short distance aways.

His partner was scared to death and refused. In the interim the fish began to do one of those death rolls sharks are famous for near the boat. It then got tail-wrapped and snapped the mono like a thread.

This was about the time the movie *Jaws* hit the silver screen, and my friend was convinced he had hooked a great white shark. At the time I believed him, but my experience in the years since has changed my mind. Based on his description, the time of year, and the situation, odds are it was a large sandbar or brown shark—a thick, large-finned, heavy-bodied fish-eating shark. Brown sharks pose little danger to humans. During hot summers they are known to invade the waters of southern New England, gravitating toward tidal estuaries, where they give live birth to their young, literally in the middle of rich food sources such as great schools of menhaden. This behavior places the newborns right in the middle of an instant food source to help them get started in their predatory existence. In the hot summer of 1995, with conditions very much like those above, a fair number of brown sharks invaded the lower Connecticut River. The first few were caught accidentally by fishermen live-lining menhaden off the breakwall for big stripers. The others, including the current Connecticut state record of 118 pounds, 7 ounces, were caught intentionally during what became a small, limited shark fishery in the shallow waters off the mouth of the Connecticut River for about a month that year, and periodically before and since. The anglers who have caught these fish now look for them when conditions are right.

This pin-hooking friend of mine was an impressively skilled big-fish specialist of a striperman. At one time or another he'd fished for everything in the sea, and he knew what was going on. I both liked and despised this guy, because of his callous behavior when it came to killing striped bass for money. And he wasn't the only one—not even close. The small army of pin hookers who targeted the adult striped bass from Maryland to Maine, combined with what was essentially unregulated harvest of small stripers in their nursery grounds in Chesapeake Bay, ultimately destroyed this incredible fishery.

It would be difficult to duplicate the massive catch from Brenton Reef that my buddy and I saw that day back in the early 1970s, because not enough of the current striped bass population has reached its full age and growth potential. Still, a good fisherman can go out and catch large numbers of 30- to 40-inchers (though not 30- to 40-pounders) at Brenton Reef and in many locations along the coast at present. The bass are back and cruising along the rocks off Brenton Reef and Brenton Point as they have done since the ice melted back thousands of years ago. This is one of the best striper-fishing destinations in the state, if not the entire region.

There are two smaller launch sites, both off Ocean Drive (one off Elm Street and Poplar Street) near Kenny's Beach, which are made of natural rock and cement. Parking is limited, but they do provide a nearly direct shot and short run to Brenton Reef from the tip of Aquidneck Island.

Downtown Newport along the famous Cliff Walk is a long, rugged, rocky shoreline that is loaded with big striped bass. It's a long haul between access points, but the fishing can be excellent all along the way. The whitewater along the perimeter of Newport is all great fishing with reasonable public access found at the state parks, all of which are strategically located on the best points and peninsulas. Parking is where you find it during the tourist season. Anglers who do the best have strong legs.

Some surf casters will start at Eastons Beach right on Route 138A, leaving their car in the parking area located at the eastern end of the beach. Eastons Beach is often referred to by local fishermen as First Beach, and as its name implies it's the first of three numbered beaches. They string off in consecutive order to the east of Newport and across the line into Middletown.

First, Second, and Third Beaches seem to heat up a tad later in spring than the places farther up inside Narragansett Bay where the water warms more easily and much sooner. When these spots do rev up for the season, however, the bass will stick around until they vacate in fall. First Beach itself often holds school bass, blues, tinker mackerel, and snapper blues in fall. It is a place that produces fish constantly through the season. Because it's a dead-end cove, however, this area often clogs up with debris, making it a difficult area to fish. As in many such locales, the best time to fish it is around the top of the tide and during the ebb.

Under low-light conditions or after dark, striped bass will move out of their deep-water hideouts and into some very shallow water in coves and along rocky shorelines to feed, wherever they are found. This typical activity pattern is governed primarily by water temperature, depth, and the presence of prey.

When there is enough water for bass to feel secure, and food is present, these beaches can become easy pickings for the anglers who learn the individual patterns for a given cove or beach—especially dead-end places that tend to run hot and cold.

Your best bet for a bigger bass is to hoof it down the Cliff Walk and cast from the rocks wherever possible. When the surf is up, this can be a slippery and dangerous area to fish, as can many of the rocky shorelines throughout New England. It may be a good idea for surf fishermen who are risk takers to wear an inflatable life vest to increase their odds of survival should they be swept off the rocks by an oddball wave or sent into the water due to a slip.

As you drive Tuckerman Avenue along the coast, two other parking areas provide access to Easton Point and its rocky shore. From First Beach, take Purgatory Road to Sachuest Point Road. Off the road is Second Sachuest Beach, or Second Beach. This is a spot where surf fishermen often stop when doing a paper route between favorite fishing holes. These beaches are all close together, making it easy to find and follow fish that are moving along a shoreline with the tides. Second Beach is probably spoken of more frequently in reports than the other two. Located on the ocean side of Sachuest Point, it too will collect debris at times, but it's swept clean by winds and tides more readily.

Follow Sachuest Point Road to the end and into Sachuest Point National Wildlife Refuge. Almost like bookends, this is the counterpart to Brenton Reef. With its rock outcrops and rocky beaches, it makes fine habitat for striped bass and other game-fish—great fishing from both the surf casting out and a boat casting in. It's also in an ideal location, protruding out into the water where the Sakonnet River empties into the Atlantic. When the tides are moving, the rip lines and currents that set up in this place are a magnet for striped bass, bluefish, tautog, and other gamefish traveling into and through the area.

Around the northeastern side of Sachuest Point—a peninsula shaped much like a foot—Third Beach lies nestled between Flint Point and the rocks to the north. It is located on Third Beach Road, a right turn out of the refuge. A parking lot at the end of this road provides excellent access to Flint Point and Third Beach.

All three of these beaches—First, Second, and Third—along with the rocky shores that connect them, are great habitats for fish. The key to good fishing is the presence of bait, whether it be sand eels, spawning worms, silversides, anchovies, or menhaden in adult or juvenile forms. Any and all of these baits will bring the fish in and hold them as long as they remain in an area.

These beaches are the kind of places where, during years of abundance, juvenile menhaden or peanut bunker get trapped by marauding predators. When this happens, you'll experience surf fishing that is as good as it gets. It's supported by what I refer to as local or resident fish, the small groups or individual fish that some how get separated from or leave the general masses and schools of fish that move into and through the region every season. When the bait moves or is pushed out, the action will turn off like a light switch.

This kind of situation occurs everywhere along the coast, especially when bunker are abundant. Small bunker draw everything from fluke to monster stripers and false albacore when they are present. This string of beaches provides the classic habitat for hot fishing action to take place on a consistent basis, especially during late summer and fall when all the small baits are dropping out of their nursery areas in rivers and estuaries farther up the bay and migrating out to the coast. This area is always great fishing, but look for it to pick up a notch or two in late summer and fall.

Moving up into the bay from the west passage, one of the more popular landmarks to fish is the Jamestown bridge. From boats, anglers fish around the pilings for striped bass and blackfish. Bluefish and false albacore are constantly on the move in season, but they'll often pass through this area with the dropping tide. The flats around the bridge are popular and productive fluke-fishing drifts.

The old Jamestown bridge is a ready-made fishing pier for shore-based anglers. Much of it is in very shallow, usually unproductive water, but out away from shore—near the channel and around the pilings—anglers fish eels after dark. Jigs and swimming plugs can also be cast around the structure, and even fluke can be caught by casting a baited jig out and dragging it slowly along the bottom, essentially creating your own drift while working it back to the shore.

Fluke and big bass can be tough or impossible to lift very far without losing them, so fishermen have invented ingenious methods for landing fish from great heights. Using a wide-mouthed basket-style net on a rope is the norm when it comes to fishing bridges and high piers successfully.

North along the West Passage, as the bay begins to divide into small coves and incoming river channels, lies Wickford Harbor. It offers little angler access, due the fact that most of the waterfront is privately owned. The primary access from shore is the North Kingston Town Beach, in downtown North Kingston. Parking is off Beach Street, a turn toward the bay off Route 1A. This is one of those dead-end kind of places that produce some schoolie bass and blues early in the season, then turn on later as small baitfish become more prevalent in the bay, drawing snapper and adult blues to within casting distance of shore.

There are two launch sites in North Kingston. One is a small, poorly marked, poorly maintained gravel launch with limited parking is located off Pleasant Street, a turn off downtown Main Street. It's hard to find, tucked between Pleasant Street Wharf and Wickford Yacht Club, and has no sign to mark it—I wonder why? This is more of a cartop or canoe drop point.

The North Kingston Town Boat Ramp is located at the end of Intrepid Drive, off Route 1 north of the police station. You'll find plenty of room for parking as well as a small dock that can be used for launch purposes only—no fishing. This is the best access to the fishing found in and around Wickford Harbor and the middle reaches of the bay. It's a fairly brief run across the bay to the east to reach the fishy waters around Prudence Island.

When fishing first starts up in spring, bluefish, squeteague, and stripers can be found in and around the harbor. As summer settles in, the bass tend to drop down the bay to cooler waters and are replaced by fluke and bluefish. The waters around the mouth of Wickford Harbor are a good spot to drift for fluke—one of those protected places that anglers can use to hide from the wind when conditions are unfavorable out in the more exposed waters of the bay or Atlantic.

The next major cove encountered while moving northward into the upper portion of Narragansett Bay is Greenwich Bay, in the city of Warwick. There are three public parks and seven launch areas of various sizes in the vicinity.

Heading north on Route 1 is Goddard State Park, a beautiful site on Greenwich Bay that offers everything from golfing to swimming. Take a right onto Forge Road and a left onto Ives Road; the entrances are off Ives Road. Besides plenty of shoreline, there is a public launch site here with ample parking for vehicles and trailers. Across the bay, the East Greenwich Town Boat Ramp is located near the municipal transfer station on Water Street off Route 1.

In the northwest corner of Greenwich Bay is Apponaug Cove, which has two launch sites. A second town launch is found here, east of the railroad tracks, just off Post Road. If this launch is full, just before it off Post Road you'll find a private marina with a launch area that can be used for a fee. Nearby at the municipal dock is parking for 60 boats and trailers. Ice, bait, and tackle are all available here.

Warwick City Park provides access to the shore for crabbing and some fishing a short distance east of Apponaug. Take Long Street off Route 117 (West Shore Road) to get there. This is a major recreation area that has waterfront access on Brush Neck Cove.

Across the cove is Seaview Beach, located on Crockett Street, a right turn off Oakland Beach Avenue. This beach has no lifeguards. It's a popular clamming spot with limited fishing potential except at high tide and after dark. In winter it may produce some winter flounder. In spring and fall stripers and bluefish occasionally push bait into this area.

At the end of Oakland Beach Road is Oakland Beach, a much better prospect for fishing. Located at the end of a point between two large coves, this is a spot that is swept by currents when the tides change—currents that carry bait and hence attract predators, especially from high slack through the end of the ebb tide.

Heading up around Warwick Point into Providence, north of the famous Rocky Point Amusement Park, anglers can fish from shore off Warwick Light as well as from areas along the coast near Rocky Point Park.

North of the park are three more launch areas. One, located at the end of Ogden Avenue Extension off Burnett Drive, is a steep, small boat launch that has no real parking area associated with it—an impractical place to fish. A short distance before Ogden Avenue is Samuel Gorton Avenue, with Long Meadow Beach at the end. Long Meadow Beach provides some shore-fishing access to the Providence River and has a launch area with parking for 25 trailers.

The best fishing and launch site in this stretch of the bay, however, is found in Conimicut Point Park. Follow Point Avenue off Route 117 to get there. This is the Shawomet Boat Ramp and Conimicut Point Light. Shore fishermen can fish from the light, the nearby beaches, and rights-of-way at Shawomet (where the launch is located) and Bellman Avenues on the north side of the point. South is the beach. You can fish in the Providence River wherever you can reach the water.

The entire area from Greenwich to Providence is heavily developed. Though there are numerous small access points to the waterfront throughout the upper portion of Narragansett Bay, there isn't much safe access from Conimicut Point to Providence. Still, a couple of access areas to the Seekonk River exist in East Providence.

At the end of Waterman Street—a turn toward the river off Blackstone Boulevard—is Blackstone Park, a 40-acre city park with 2,400 feet of waterfront access. At its south end is additional parking with limited fishing access at the Richmond Square parking lot.

Farther north up the east side of the Seekonk River on School Street—a right toward the water while heading south on Route 114—is the School Street Pier. Called the State Dock by locals, the pier provides angler access to the river, though parking is limited to roadside parking spaces.

Farther north, below the Division Street bridge off Taft Street, is the Pawtucket Town Boat Launch—another small area in a tough part of town, with limited parking. Not a formula for a perfect outing. This is a dangerous a place primarily used by locals.

These access points in the upper bay around Providence and up inside the Providence and Seekonk Rivers are certainly not "go-to" fishing areas. They provide limited potential for success if you're targeting striped bass in spring and fall. In late winter and very early spring, around ice-out, when winter flounder spawn, there used to be (no recent reliable reports) some short periods of fishing for winter flounder. In summer bluefish and snapper blues will feed their way up inside the bay while pushing bait up into places such as this. Look for the best fishing to be at high water and under low-light conditions. Again, all these downtown places provide very limited access to not-so-productive fishing waters that are largely polluted, in a bad part of a city area.

As you head south along the east side of Narragansett Bay out of Providence, the area becomes more suburban in the towns of Barrington and Warren. There are numerous marinas in this area, though public access is limited. A right turn off Route 114 onto Wheaton Street leads to the Warren Town Launch on the Warren River. The nearby town beach provides limited angler access during off-hour and off-season periods. Fishing will be for some winter flounder early and late in the year, school bass, and bluefish during late summer when they feed their way for miles into all the area's estuaries and rivers. Bristol, to the south, offers a couple of small launch sites.

By far the best access to the water in the northeastern portion of Narragansett Bay is Colt State Park in the town of Bristol, off Route 117. Colt State Park has a variety of habitats to play in. You'll find a small salt marsh that connects to the bay along its western shore. An excellent concrete launch site with ample parking lies in the northwest corner of the park, near the salt marsh. There is also a dock at the ferry landing, which runs summertime excursions to nearby Prudence Island. This dock lets you cast into slightly deeper waters that are more likely to hold desirable fish. The best asset, however, is the boat launch, which offers a decent point from which to attack the often productive north end of Prudence Island.

Colt Park is located on a large peninsula west across Bristol Harbor. In downtown Bristol is the State Pier and Boat Launch Area at the end of State Street, near the Bristol Town Boat Launch. Unfortunately, parking is limited to town residents with stickers.

On the Mount Hope Bay side of Bristol are two small shore-based fishing access areas with limited parking. Off Route 136 (Metacom Avenue) is Annawamscutt Drive, at the end of which lies a paved right-of-way down a steep bank. Below is a cobble beach that will produce striped bass, weakfish, bluefish, snapper blues, and occasional winter or summer flounder. From there you can walk south down the beach to the Mount Hope Fishing Access Area, located at the end of Narrows Road.

Upper Narragansett Bay is better explored via boat than shore access points, which are limited in number and provide only fair to moderately good fishing once they are found.

The upper portion of the bay is a very complex system of inflowing rivers, tide marshes, points, islands, and bars. Much of the water is shallow, making navigation difficult at low tide.

Because this area is very shallow, it warms much more quickly in spring than the surrounding ocean waters, bringing forage species and worm spawns to life in late April or early May. The upper bay initially provides some limited early-season fishing for striped bass that overwintered in the various protected spots and around warm-water discharges in the Providence area. There are also small numbers of winter flounder that enter the bay to spawn in fall and leave once water temps get much above 50 degrees.

Weakfish, early-run stripers, and the first bluefish caught in this part of the world are usually taken from these warmer waters of upper Narragansett Bay. Fluke move up into the deeper areas such as Wickford Harbor and Greenwich Bay. They provide some decent fishing throughout the summer, with some bluefish and schoolie bass often present around structures that create rip and current lines. Larger stripers tend to move up into the bay early, when temps are cool and bait plentiful. The bay offers a May worm spawn similar to what you'll find in the salt ponds to the south, which creates quite a stir when it is taking place. As the waters warm, the fish drop down to the cool, comfortable waters around Newport and Jamestown, or head out into the Atlantic and swing to the north.

When juvenile bunker and other superabundant bait sources move into the bay in late summer and fall, they attract the same menu of fish back inside, where they rummage around for food until cooling fall temperatures force them out into the ocean. A few striped bass don't leave, but move into protected areas of the bay to spend the winter.

Prudence Island is the largest of the numerous islands in Narragansett Bay. Boat anglers will want to fish the rocks and ledges around its perimeter for bass, blues, weakfish, and false albacore if or when they arrive during the fall. The north side of Prudence Island and, to the west, Sally Point are two of the places in the upper bay that consistently produce weakfish after the early-spring period of comparatively fast fishing slows down. These fish move around and are caught occasionally throughout most of the bay, but seem to settle into certain areas, occasionally up inside bays and rivers for a while.

Heading south through the narrows between Mount Hope Bay and the Sakonnet River is a large, nearly oval salt pond called the Cove. Off Route 138 in the Cove is a run-down state launch with a single concrete slab. Used mostly by clammers and bird-watchers, it does provide access to both the Sakonnet River and Mount Hope Bay.

South off Route 138 on Jummock Avenue is the old Stone Bridge, located at the end of Point Road. This place was the old abutment for the original bridge between Portsmouth and Tiverton, on the east side of the Sakonnet River. It was partially destroyed by Hurricane Carol in 1954, and the old abutment has been made into a fishing pier. Nearby is a parking area with a small marina and boat ramp near the bridge. Farther south lies Teddy's Beach, which is accessible via Park Avenue off Point Road. Parking in these areas is limited but reasonable.

These are excellent tide-swept areas that hold and attract all the species of fish that frequent the bay. The narrow constriction in this area increases tidal velocities, making it an excellent place to fish either from shore or from a boat. Naturally, the new bridge abutments are striped bass magnets that should always be checked out if you're in the area with a boat. This is the kind of classic structure that begs for some vertical jigging or live eels fished deep after dark. The flushing action here makes the waters clear and cleaner than in the upper bay, where eelgrass and other debris may collect in slow-water areas; it's difficult to fish effectively when the water is full of such trash.

Across the Sakonnet River, on the east bank at the end of Seapowet Avenue (a turn toward the Sakonnet off Route 77 in Tiverton), lies Seapowet Marsh and Fishing Area. The junction of the marsh and Sakonnet River creates a productive area for anglers who want to work the shores.

Farther south along the river, near the junction of Fogland Road and High Hill Avenue, is another small access area with a broken-down launch that may not be suitable for boats with trailers. Parking is limited, but you will find ample space at the Tiverton Town Beach about a quarter mile away, making it a walk-and-fish destination. You can fish from the beach in the off season.

As you head into Sakonnet Harbor, you'll find a small concrete launch cutting across a beach. This launch is off Sakonnet Point Road at the end of Route 77, and it provides excellent small-boat access to the lower Sakonnet River, Sakonnet Point, and the great whitewater along the beaches at the tip of Aquidneck Island in Newport.

At the mouth of the harbor is a breakwall that provides a popular shore-based fishing access; it's at the end of Bluffhead Road off Sakonnet Point Road. The best and most picturesque fishing place in this area is Sakonnet Point itself, a boulder-strewn spot that begs to be fished and harbors some big striped bass during the course of the season. Both Sakonnet Point and the more protected breakwall are a good shore-fishing spots from which to cast an eel after dark for the big ones. The area also gets plenty of play from bluefish, tautog, scup, and fluke. The mouth of the Sakonnet River is a great spot to target big striped bass and doormat fluke.

To the east, right on the Massachusetts line, is Little Compton Town Beach, or South Shore Beach. It can be reached by heading east on Swamp Road off Route 77. Swamp Road turns into Brownell Road; take a right from Brownell onto South Shore Road and follow it to the beach. Right near the state border, Tunipus Pond and nearby Quicksand Salt Pond both dump into the ocean along this beach, with the larger Quicksand Pond at its eastern edge. Both are prime places to cast a lure or bait, especially early and late in the year when the warmer waters from the pond will attract and hold predators that wait for bait to be pulled out with the tides.

South Shore Beach is right on the cold waters of the Atlantic, with a beautiful view of the Elizabeth Islands off Cape Cod. This picturesque spot produces early migratory striped bass and bluefish in spring, plus fluke and porgies later in summer when water temps warm up. Try casting a mummichog with a 3-inch-long squid strip on a tiny jig for fluke off the salt pond mouths on an ebb tide by day, or eels and plugs at dawn and dusk for bass. Big bass are caught in this area every year. Due to heavy beach traffic, the area is best approached during off hours or in spring and fall, when beachgoers are less abundant.

INDEX